The Fossil Diggings on Wicken Fen

Bernard O'Connor

Bernard O'Connor

Few visitors to Wicken Fen, even many of the residents of the rural communities in the Cambridgeshire fens, know of this area's role in the development of an industry of world importance. In the second part of the nineteenth century vast fortunes were made from the digging up, washing, transporting and processing of what were called "coprolites", thought at the time to be fossilised droppings of fish, lizards and even dinosaurs! Many of the Cambridge Colleges, their professors and students, Cambridge surveyors and solicitors like Bidwell and Francis, local land-owning families and the clergy were very much involved in this unique and fascinating business and its from examination of their archives that I have been able to piece together an account of the social, religious and economic impact that this unusual industry had on Wicken and surrounding parishes.

I have to acknowledge the research work done by David Short of Ashwell Field Studies Centre, Betty Wooton, Richard Grove, Walter Tye, Albert Sheldrick and Audrey Kiln. The Masters, Fellows, Students at King's College and St. John's College Cambridge very kindly provided me with access to their archives. I would also like to acknowledge the assistance of the staff at the following institutions: -

Cambridgeshire County Record Office,
Hertfordshire County Record Office,
The Cambridge Collection, Cambridge,
Cambridge University Library,
Cambridge Folk Museum,
Sedgwick Museum, Cambridge,
The Public Record Office, Kew,
The Valence House Museum, Dagenham,
Church Commissioners' Record Office, London,
Charity Commissioners' Record Office, London.

Many others in the area have given snippets of information and encouragement but it is to the memory of those who worked in the diggings that this book is dedicated.

Bernard O'Connor

In 1846 a new industry started in the fens between Burwell and Wicken, small farming communities about twelve miles north-east of Cambridge. It provided a very different occupation to agricultural work, that of coprolite digging and locally called "fossiling." Until the nineteenth century Wicken was a small agricultural parish that had hardly changed since the Middle Ages. In 1801 the population was 614. Fifty years later it had increased almost 40% to 1,054. This was despite some families moving elsewhere in search of work. The parish enclosure at the turn of the century led many land workers to lose their right to graze on the common land. Some left the parish to find work in the towns. Improved health care reduced the death rate and there was a strong tradition of large families in the 19th century. Ten children were not uncommon. There were also strong feelings about social inequality that resulted in a high crime rate and significant out-migration. But beyond the rural communities of Cambridgeshire there were dramatic changes taking place.

The 18th and 19th century exodus from the countryside to the urban areas resulted in an enormous demand for accommodation and food. The ending of the Napoleonic Wars with the defeat of the French at Waterloo in 1815 brought a period of peace and prosperity to Britain. Its population doubled over the first half of the century. Towns and cities expanded rapidly on the coalfields and alongside the major rivers, railways and canals. People were attracted by the employment opportunities in industry, retail and commerce following the inventions of the Industrial Revolution.

There were also many forced off the land by developments in the Agricultural Revolution. The urban population needed feeding. The typical two-up two-down terraced houses did not have the gardens to grow fruit or vegetables or space to keep a pig or chickens. People needed to buy food from the High Street, the market or the corner shops. Victorian entrepreneurs were quick to recognise the growing demand. Small family businesses dominated the business. As their profits grew they rented more market stalls, opened more shops, invested in better transport and had more money to buy from the farmers. If farmers could increase production there was more money to be made. Experiments began in an attempt to increase food production.

One can probably remember from one's schooldays Jethro Tull's seed drill, Lord 'Turnip' Townsend's four-course crop rotation method and the Earl of Leicester and other agriculturalists' experiments at crossbreeding to produce bigger and better pigs, cattle and sheep. But other experiments were going on with plants. The application of science and capital was being expended on agriculture as it had been on manufacturing. Once the chemists acknowledged that phosphate was a major nutrient in plant growth, the search was on to discover new supplies. In 1828 a rock phosphate, called phosphorite, started being exploited in Ontario, Canada. Chemists had found its value as a fertiliser and samples were tested in Great Britain. The German explorer, Alexander Von Humboldt, returned to Europe with details of the South American coastline and his report led to the European's "discovering" the use of "huano" or guano. This was an accumulation of tens of feet of phosphate-rich bird droppings that had impregnated discarded fish carcasses and bird skeletons on the Chincha Islands off the coast of Peru. The locals would not excavate it because of the smell. So indentured Chinese labour was shipped over and forced to work. Shipping companies started to import guano into Liverpool docks from 1838 where it was sold it at up to £12 per ton. This was much more expensive than bones, the then popular fertiliser, but a successful advertising campaign in the agricultural press led to its widespread usage.

Other experiments included adding a whole range of materials to the soil. Bones, blood, soot, fish, seaweed, chalk, clay and even rags from discarded wool and cotton clothes were trialled. Maybe one can remember the rag and bone man? It was the waste product of the knife manufacturers in Sheffield, however, that sparked the interest in bones. It was found that the shavings from their knife handles proved a very effective fertiliser when added to the soil. (Voelcker, A. (1862), 'The International Exhibition at Paris,' p.149) The corn mills used by the agricultural suppliers were not able to meet the demand for bone meal and this led to the setting up of bone manure works. Their most popular products were half-inch bones. These were burnt or crushed and added to the soil as bone meal. It can be bought today at your local garden centre.

However, the bones from the knacker's yards were insufficient to meet the demand of the nation's manure manufacturers, a factor that led to the import of dried bones. There were reports of cargoes of mummified cats from Egyptian pyramids and sun-bleached bones from the battlefields of Europe, the North African desert and the Argentinean Pampas finding their way into the crushing mills. This was enough to prompt the comment by Baron Von Justus Liebig, that,

> "Great Britain is like a ghoul, searching the continents for bones to feed its agriculture ... robbing all other countries of the condition of her fertility. Already in her eagerness for bones she has turned up the battlefields of Leipzig, Waterloo, and of the Crimea; already from the catacombs of Sicily she has carried away the skeletons of many successive generations."

(Quoted in Keatley, W. S. (1976), '100 years of Fertiliser Manufacture,' Fertiliser Manufacturers Association; also in Pierre, W.H. and Norman, A.G. (Eds.) (1953), 'Soil Fertiliser Phosphorous in Crop Nutrition,' New York Academic Press, p. ix)

By 1839 the bone business was worth £150,000 per annum and about 30,000 tons were being imported annually. The Gardeners' Chronicle and Agricultural Gazette gave detailed accounts of the efficacy of these new manures. (Graham, J. (1839), 'A Treatise on the Use and Value of Manure', London p.6) However, tests showed that crushed bones were insoluble. It took a long time before their mineral potential could be absorbed by the plant roots. Bones were expensive and the machinery for grinding them had not been perfected. (Ibid.)

Life in the agricultural communities where these new ideas were being practised was not the quiet and peaceful rural idyll that characterised traditional images of country life. There were tremendous economic and social changes brought about in the nineteenth century. The introduction of the Enclosures after 1799 and the implementation of the new technology introduced during the "Agricultural Revolution" had a dramatic impact on rural villages. Many farm labourers became entirely dependent of the farmers for their livelihood. There were "hiring fairs" where men and women were taken on according to the decorations in their lapels. The historian, David Ellison, commented on the "startling" social effects that resulted.

> "*The repeal of the Corn Laws and the lower prices of corn for farmers had made them all try to save costs by mechanisation and reducing their labour forces... Cambridge's farm labourers had often noticed the immense gulf between themselves with their £25 to £30 a year, and the rectors with £300 - £400, comfortable rectories, and often land as well as house servants.*"

(Ellison, D. 'Coprolites in the Orwell area,' part of Orwell history topics; Ref. Latter Day Saints Millennial Star, passim, and Kowallis, Gay P. (1970?), 'To the Great Salt Lake from Litlington,' Bassingbourn)

Farm labourers were often provided with a tied cottage from which they could easily be evicted at the whim of the farmer or farm bailiff. Not being seen at church for the Sunday service was a dismissible offence. Going into the public house before the farmer and farm bailiff arrived after church was unwise. Crowds waited at the door in deference. There was considerable poverty and overcrowding in crumbling "shit and stubble" or wattle and daub thatched cottages in many rural villages. New steam-powered agricultural machinery, designed to save time and labour, was introduced by farmers who were keen to profit from the increased demand for food. These machines like the steam traction engine, threshing machine, deep plough and elevator resulted in an increasing number of redundancies in farm labour. Some people developed useful mechanical skills but there was widespread unrest in most rural communities. Many landless peasants were forced off the land when they lost the right to use the open fields. The loss of gleaning rights after harvest, the loss of the common for grazing animals and poultry, the denial of access to the newly fenced or walled in woodland reduced their "free" catch of rabbit, pheasant, partridge, nuts, mushrooms and wild fruit. Poaching was punished by transportation or hanging for a second offence and man traps were common.

The more motivated sections of the community, mainly young adult males and females, left the countryside to find employment in the industrial towns and cities where better paid factory or domestic work was available. Some were attracted by the numerous advertisements in the Cambridge Chronicle, Cambridge Independent Press and the Royston Crow to emigrate. Hard working, temperate labourers and craftsmen were offered employment and land in the colonies in Canada, South Africa, Australia and New Zealand. But it was another enterprise that halted this out-migration and very much brought this area into the Victorian era of industrial and economic change. Most of the villagers were engaged as agricultural labourers on the local farms and large estates or were employed as domestics in some of the country houses of the gentry. Wealthier landowners lived in larger properties like Burwell House, Bottisham Hall, Bendyshe Hall, Anglesey Abbey and Eye Hall, which had large gardens and often parkland. They employed large numbers of domestic servants, nursery maids, governesses, gardeners, grooms and coachmen. The majority of the villagers lived in small, cramped, single-storey thatched, cottages made of clunch, rough chalk cut from local pits,. They often had an outside washhouse and a small garden for growing fruit and vegetables and kept a pig and chickens.

When the families got together at Easter and Christmas for baptisms, marriages and funerals, stories of the changes in rural and urban life would have been common. With improvements in education and increases in the numbers of pamphlets, newspapers and journals there was a growing awareness of the disparity between town and countryside. For those who were unable to leave, some manifested their dissatisfaction with the state of affairs by acts of vandalism. This period, known as "The Swing" after the number of hangings of offenders, saw incidences of farm machinery being destroyed and haystacks, barns and even farmers' houses being set alight. (Fowle, K. (1992), 'Coton through the Ages') However, the discovery of a fossil seam reduced this unrest.

As shall be seen, this dissatisfaction diminished during the coprolite years with higher wages and a variety of new jobs available. What were these coprolites? "Coprolites," as they were called when they were first discovered, were thought to be fossilised droppings. Analysis of the 1861 to 1891 census returns shows that there were numerous variations of their spelling, due in part to the poor literacy of the census enumerator but also to variations in local dialect. They include coprolite, copperlight, copper light, copperlite, coupperlite, copralite, corporolite, coprelite, coperlite, coporlite, coparlite, coprolithe and coperalite. No wonder there was confusion over their origin.

The word came from the Greek "kopros" meaning dung and "lithos" meaning stone. Dung stone - fossilised droppings! Rev. William Buckland, the Dean of Westminster, coined it when he was the first professor of Geology and Mineralogy at the University of Oxford. In 1829 he went on a geological excursion to the Dorset coast at Lyme Regis. Examining the clay and sands exposed by a recent landslip he found the complete fossil remains of an ichthyosaurus. Unusually, it also included its fossilised stomach contents.

Accompanying him on the excursion was the German analytical chemist, Baron Von Justus Liebig. He too was fascinated with the finds but the Dean was obsessed. He had slices made of them so he could examine them under a microscope. He had a tabletop inlaid with polished sections as well as earrings made from polished slices! It is unknown whether he wore them! His dinner parties were very entertaining. A bear used to wander around the dining room behind his guests and a monkey sat on furniture near the window. The menu often included samples from across the food chain, starting from plants and working through the animal kingdom! The worst tasting were reportedly moles and bluebottles! Dinnertime conversations included a challenge to the established religious circles. Buckland had found tiny bones of baby ichthyosaurus in the coprolites. This meant that ichthyosaurus ate ichthyosaurus. They were cannibals! This contradicted the fundamental religious belief that life before Adam was one of peace and harmony. Some argued that Adam and Eve frolicked with dinosaurs in Eden. Maybe the issue was discussed over dinner with Mr and Mrs Mantell who were the first to find iguanodon remains in Sussex in 1822 and Sir Richard Owen who first came up with the word dinosaur to mean "terrible lizard". Owen was just as eccentric. On New Year's Eve 1853 he invited twenty scientists to a dinner party inside a life-size model of an iguanodon in a London park!

A similar discovery but one with far reaching implications was made in 1842. After Rev. John Henslow, the professor of Botany at St. John's College, Cambridge had been given a living by St. John's in the Suffolk parish of Hitcham, he went on a trip to the Victorian watering hole of Felixstowe. There had recently been a landslip in which he found some interesting fossils in the newly exposed Suffolk Crag at the bottom of the cliffs. There were loads of them. From their smooth, brown, elongated shape he took them to be fossilised dung, similar to those of the ichthyosaurus, discovered by Buckland. (O'Connor, B. (1998), 'Felixstowe's Fossil Industry', Everton) He suspected that, like animal manure, they would be useful as a manure once they were ground to a powder. He was probably aware from reading about Suffolk's history that the Crag had been used on the fields for generations. In Walter

Tye's research into the origins of the coprolite industry he noted that

> "A Suffolk farmer first discovered the fertilizing value of the Suffolk red crag. I prefer that John Kirby, (Suffolk Traveller,1764) of Wickham Market, should tell the story in his own inimitable way :-
>
> "In a Farmers Yard in Levington, clofe on the left as you enter from Levington into the faid Chapel Field of Stratton Hall, was dug the firft Crag of Shell that have been found ufeful for improving the land in this and other Hundreds in the neighbourhood. For though it appears from Books of Agriculture, that the like manure has long been ufeful in the Weft of England, it was not ufed here till this Difcovery was cafually made by one Edmund Edwards, about the year 1718. This man, being covering a Field with Muck out of his yard, and wanting a load of two to finifh it, carried fome of the Soil that laid near the Muck, tho' it looked to him no better than Sand; but obferving the Crop to be beft where he laid that, he was from thence encouraged to carry more of it the next year; and the success he had, encouraged others to do the like." There is no need for me to explain that Edmund Edwards' discovery was soon broadcast throughout south-east Suffolk, where the crag was found. Large quantities were very soon carried and scattered over the heaths and sheep-walks, where the soil had always been hungry and inadequately fed."

(Walter Tye, 'Birth of Fertilizer Industry, 1930, Fison's Journal, p.4.)

Liebig had done some tests on Buckland's coprolites by dissolving them in vitriol, the term then used for sulphuric acid. His analysis of the resultant mass showed them to have a high phosphate content, a mineral much needed in plant growth. John Bennet Lawes, a Hertfordshire landowner, was experimenting with different manures on his estate in Rothamsted. Like Liebig, he too successfully dissolved animal bones, the mineral phosphorite and Felixstowe coprolites in vitriol. The resulting mixture, once dried and bagged, he called "super phosphate of lime". His tests showed that it was soluble in water and that the plant roots could absorb it much more rapidly than bone meal. He experimented with it on plants in pots and test beds and found it to be an extremely effective manure, especially for root crops. He called it "super" and realised that it was the world's first artificial chemical manure. Its application would so dramatically increase turnip yields that it would be much in demand by the nation's farmers. They were eager to improve supplies of winter fodder. This was because once the harvest was in and farmers knew how much fodder was available over winter, large numbers of surplus cattle, sheep or pigs had to be slaughtered. Meat commanded higher prices over winter until the new stock was brought onto the market in spring. Any way of providing increased fodder therefore would be very popular with farmers.

Much to Lawes' pleasure the results of his tests with his new manure showed that it was effective on a whole range of other crops. He patented his "discovery" in 1842, which annoyed Liebig who claimed to have been the first to do it. It also upset Lawes' mother who was appalled that a gentleman should engage in trade - let alone in manure. Ignoring both he set up his own company. It was called "Lawes Artificial Manure Company." His fiancée could not have been pleased. The planned European Tour for their honeymoon was cancelled in favour of a trip down the Thames during which he spotted an ideal site for his factory. He bought a plot at Deptford and had a large chemical manure works built that was capable of producing up to 200 tons of superphosphate a week. He sold his "super" at up to £7.00 a ton and took legal action against Liebig and others to ensure that anyone who wanted to use his patent had to pay him five shillings (£0.25) for every ton they produced. (Dyke, G.V. (1993), 'John Lawes of Rothamsted' Hoos Press, Harpenden, p.15)

Maybe Henslow was in correspondence with Lawes as he realised that the Felixstowe fossil bed could be a valuable source of manure. As a wide range of animal manure was being put onto the fields he thought that fossilised droppings could be used for the same purpose. In 1845 he read a paper in Cambridge to the British Association for the Advancement of Science. (Henslow, Rev. John, (1845), Report to British Association, Cambridge) It dealt with their potential value to the nation's farmers. Suffolk manure manufacturers like William Colchester, Edward Packard and Joseph Fison took interest. They made arrangements with Felixstowe landowners to have the fossils dug up, washed and transported to their works in Ipswich. A few shillings a ton royalty was offered for the fossils. As a cheap alternative to the other manures on the market, there was keen interest in coprolites.

Maybe it was the reports of Rev. Henslow's speech that prompted a local farmer to show him some fossils that he had dug up on his property. Charles Kingsley, one of Henslow's students, must have been present as he recorded Henslow's response.

> "He saw, being somewhat of, a geologist and chemist, that they were not, as fossils usually are, carbonate of lime, but phosphate of lime - bone earth. He said at once, as by inspiration, "You have found a treasure - not a gold-mine, indeed, but a food-mine. This bone earth, which we are at our wit's end to get for our grain and pulses; which we are importing, as expensive bones, all the way from Buenos Ayres. Only find enough of them, and you will increase immensely the food supply of England and perhaps make her independent of foreign phosphates in case of war."
>
> (Anonymous note in Ipswich Museum's Coprolite file)

A treasure? A food-mine? Such a response must have astounded the farmer. It is undocumented where the farmer was from but it is thought that he was from Burwell. Fossils had been found beneath the fenland peat from as early as 1816. (Hailstone, Rev. J. (1816), 'Outlines of the Geology of Cambridgeshire', Phil. Trans. Royal. Soc., pp.243-250) Their discovery was related to an important fenland occupation, locally called "claying". This involved the digging of small pits through the "moor" or "bear's muck", as the bog-earth was called, to reach the clay. This lay between two and ten feet (0.74m. - 3.7m.) below the surface. Wearing waterproofed boots the diggers would use a sharp, cutting-edged shovel to dig through the peat, a light wooden scoop to get rid of drainage water and an axe or "bill" to excavate the clay beneath. The top few feet of clay was thrown to the sides of the pit and then mixed into the peat.

The material turned up by this "claying" occasionally included fossils of what were thought to be bears and oxen. When Burwell Fen started to be drained in the early-1800s the excavation of drainage ditches or "lodes" exposed an extensive bed of fossils. A local farmer, John Ball, noticed that the turnips he grew on the clayey, fossil deposit that had been mixed into his peat soil produced dramatically better yields than the crops on fields he had not clayed. The Burwell doctor, Mr Lucas, explained that the "extraordinary liveliness" was related to the high phosphate content of the fossils. ('The Farming of Cambridgeshire,' Royal Agric.Soc.1847, p.71; Lucas, C. (1930), 'The Fenman's World - Memories of a Fenland Physician,' (Norwich), p.25)

Dr. Lucas may well have heard about Rev. Henslow's Cambridge speech or read about it in the local press. Aware of the potential demand by manure manufacturers and maybe even knowing the farmer who had shown Henslow the fossils, he suspected that the Burwell deposit could also be a matter of "commercial proposition". Their shallow depth beneath the fenland peat just above the gault clay would allow them to be raised without very high labour costs. The proximity of Burwell Lode would allow easy access by barge or lighter to Popes Corner - the confluence of the Ouse and the Cam - and then via Ely, Littleport and Downham Market onto King's Lynn where it could then transhipped to manure works in Ipswich or London.

With an eye for speculation and without having first seen it, he bought some eleven acres of Burwell Poor's Fen. The locals thought he had taken leave of his senses. A month later, so the story goes, he went by boat up Burwell Lode with "an interested party" to locate the deposit. After rowing for some time, they reached a point about a mile west of the village where the potential buyer was handed a "sprit" and told to push it into the land below the boat. (Gathercole, A. F. (1959), 'Fenland Village,' Fisons Journal, No.64 Sept. pp.24-9; Suffolk County Record Office (SCRO) HC 438.8728/269)

The depth of the seam was not noted but the locals were astounded when he sold the plot and the coprolites beneath it for £1,000. Realising almost £100 per acre was a phenomenal profit, given that agricultural rents ranged at that time from about ten to forty shillings (£0.50 - £2.00) an acre. The "interested party" was William Colchester, one of the Suffolk manure manufacturers who also had investments in brick manufacturing and ships. In 1846 he expanded his manure business by building a new manure works in Ipswich. According to a later geological paper he had raised 500 tons by 1847. (Lucas, C. (1930), op.cit; Reid, C. (1890), 'Nodule Bed,' Memoirs of the Geological Survey (MGS) p.16)

Others speculated in the new industry. Edward Packard, a chemist from Saxmundham in Suffolk successfully processed the Felixstowe "coprolites" and in 1847 he opened his own manure factory on the banks of the River Orwell in Ipswich. Joseph Fison, part of a milling and baking family, had moved into Ipswich in 1840. He established a factory at Stoke Bridge and converted it to process coprolites and other phosphatic material in 1850. (Fisons Journal, No.77, December 1963; Norsk Hydro file, Museum of East Anglian Life, Stowmarket)

Lawes, Colchester, Packard and Fison advertised their superphosphate in the pages of the "Gardeners Chronicle and Agricultural Gazette" and the "Mark Lane Express" thus realising Henslow's idea. Articles on its successful application and of using coprolites in its manufacture appeared in the agricultural press. These increased landowners and agriculturalists' awareness of the financial advantages of locating the fossil deposit on their properties.

So, by the 1850s, Rev. Buckland realised that his discovery had led to the birth of a new industry exploiting fossil beds in Suffolk and Cambridgeshire. He questioned the possibility that these

> "...excretions of extinct animals contained the mineral ingredients of so much value in animal manure. The question was in fact not yet solved by the chemist, and we took specimens, in order to confirm by chemical analysis the views of the geologist. After Liebig had completed their analysis, he saw that they might be made applicable to practical purposes.
>
> What a curious and interesting subject for contemplation! In the remains of an extinct animal world England is to find the means of increasing her wealth in agricultural produce, as she has already found the great support of her manufacturing industry in fossil fuel - the preserved matter of primeval forests - the remains of a vegetable world! May this expectation be realised! and may her excellent population be thus redeemed from poverty and misery!
>
> I well recollect the storm of ridicule raised by these expressions of the German philosopher, and

yet truth has triumphed over scepticism, and thousands of tons of similar animal remains are now used in promoting the fertility of our fields. The geological observer, in his search after evidences of ancient life, aided by the chemist, excavated extinct remains which produced new life to future generations."

(Anonymous author, 'The Study of Abstract Science Essential to the Progress of Industry,' Memoirs of Geological Survey, Mineral Statistics, vol. i, 1850?, pp.40-1)

Many people thought that the fossils were the droppings of bear, lizard, fish and even dinosaur. A retired major from Reach thought that they resembled sun-dried wildebeest droppings. They were similar to those he had seen on the flood plains of the River Zambezi once the vast herds had passed. Students and professors at Cambridge University's newly established Geology department became very interested in the range of fossils being thrown up. There was extensive debate in geological circles and many argued that the deposit ought not to be termed coprolite. They should more correctly be termed pseudo-coprolites or phosphatic nodules. However, the trade name "coprolites" stuck. Recently however, an excellent example of some poor creature's rectal content has been found in Barrington that gives credence to the locals' views. One can make out the pressure creases and a sharp point as if it was its last squeeze.

The bulk of the deposit was of misshapen, black/grey lumps but amongst them were found the teeth, bones, scales and claws of Jurassic and Cretaceous dinosaurs. They included craterosaurus, dakosaurus, dinotosaurus, megalosaurus, iguanodon and the pterodactyl. Prehistoric marine reptiles of ichthyosaurus, plesiosaurus and pliosaurus were found as well as the remains of whale, shark, turtle and a huge variety of shells, sponges and other marine organisms. The most common was the ammonite. Other animals that were discovered in the diggings included crocodiles, hippopotamus, elephant, rhinoceros, lion, hyena, tapir, bear, horse and oxen - evidence of this area's tropical past. It is thought that the mammal fossils were "discovered" when the diggers cut through much more recent sediments to reach the far more ancient Greensand sediments further down. (O'Connor, B. (1998), 'The Dinosaurs on Sandy Heath', Everton) There were also lumps of what some argue are inorganic calcium phosphate. But why is it that such a variety of creatures that you would normally expect to see in hot tropical countries in Africa were found in Cambridgeshire?

When the European plate broke away from Pangaea about 500 million years ago it was south of the Equator. It was during this period that the gault clay was deposited. This area was about 28° S, where Namibia is today! To reach its present latitude this area has moved over 80° of the planet's surface, thousands of miles. It experienced a range of differing environments on its slow movement north from the tropical and equatorial forests, swamps, savannah grassland and desert to today's temperate latitudes about 55° N. But what had produced such an enormous prehistoric graveyard? A number of the Victorian geologists considered that the Jurassic and Cretaceous fossil deposits had been washed out of the clays which were exposed when the south of England was uplifted from the sea to produce the Weald. A recent theory is that between 96 and 94 million years ago the earth experienced intense, sustained and violent asteroid bombardments. Even 10,000 kilometres away from the impact zone it has been estimated that wind speeds would have been over 100 kilometres an hour for up to 14 hours and temperature increases of over 30°C would have wiped out anything in the way. Tsunamis, massive tidal waves up to 30 metres high would have devastated land organisms. (Spedicato, E. (1990), 'Apollo Objects, Atlantis and the Deluge: A Catastrophical Scenario for the End of the Last Glaciation', Quaderni Del Dipartimento di Mathematica, Statistica, Informatica e Applicazioni, Begamo, p.10) Sea levels rose dramatically, flooding the London-Brabant Basin, of which present day Cambridgeshire formed its northern coast. This wiped out much of the animal population. Carbon dioxide given off by the flood basalts released by the tectonic activity also played their part. Many of the land creatures would have been poisoned and also the marine life that had to come up to the surface for air. Some suggested that as the bodies accumulated as debris in coastal embayments their bones, teeth, scales and claws gradually absorbed the phosphoric acid from overlying deposits of decaying organisms. Another theory was that the calcium absorbed dissolved phosphate from the seawater. It was said that the rivers had dissolved the apatite, a phosphatic mineral found in the volcanic rocks of Scandinavia and Scotland, which impregnated the deposit and explains their higher phosphate content than today's animal and human bones.

Analysis of amber samples shows that at the time when dinosaurs were at their greatest size, about 230 million years ago, the oxygen content of the air was 35%. Over the Cretaceous period it gradually declined as a result of the increased carbon dioxide released into the atmosphere by extensive volcanic activity. Levels fell to 11% 65 million years ago and today they are 21%. Dinosaurs had to adapt to these changing conditions. It was like having asthma, not getting enough oxygen into the blood. They had to build enough energy to catch prey - the "dash and dine" characteristic of today's crocodiles. Many were exhausted, maybe too tired for sex even. Like crocodiles they buried their eggs. It is thought that increased temperatures meant that they had single-sex populations that further reduced numbers. The leathery skin of their eggs absorbed the poisonous gases and embryos failed to develop. In order to survive these changing conditions dinosaurs had to evolve with a much-reduced size. A cataclysmic catastrophe like a rise in sea level of hundreds of feet as well as poisoned air could explain the huge numbers of creatures found in the East Anglian fossil beds. Given the volume of the creatures, they must have piled up on each other into a layer many tens of feet thick in hollows on the seabed. The upper bodies would have been eaten by any of the surviving marine life like ammonites and worms but the lower bodies, without oxygen for decomposition, gradually fossilised as the upper layers were covered in the hundreds of feet of Cambridgeshire Greensand. This was probably washed into the ocean from the arid parts of the continent still above sea level.

Compressed by this strata and the subsequent chalk marl of Eastern and Southern Cambridgeshire they gradually fossilised. This could explain why there are real coprolites in the deposit. The contents of stomachs, intestines and rectums would have been found along with bones, teeth, claws, scales and shells. Throughout the deposit were found large numbers of ammonites, squid-like creatures that scavenged on the sea floor but there were oyster shells on the upper surface. Over the millions of years, fluctuations in sea level exposed the soft Greensand and differential erosion uncovered the fossils at its base. The remains would have been washed around, so that one does not find whole skeletons in the deposit. Many of the surface features of the remains were removed by abrasion but lines showing worm tracks are often visible along the nodules, the biggest of which rarely extend over six inches (15cms).

Further inundation resulted in a second bed accumulating which was covered once more with Greensand deposits and then hundreds of feet of chalk. This latter deposit was made up from minute marine organisms whose bodies contained calcium carbonate. When sea levels eventually fell these more recent deposits were exposed the to the elements. The upper layers would have been eroded and the chalk and sand gradually lowered to expose the fossil beds. The sixteen ice ages contributed most to the erosion removing hundreds of feet of rock to leave the low chalk and sandy ridges of East Anglia.

Whilst the bed was one of great fascination to the country's geologists, its commercial value was not in how much they could be sold to those Victorians fascinated by fossils. Another of Rev. Henslow's students at Cambridge was Charles Darwin. His evolutionary theories caused a storm when they were published in 1858 and further stimulated the enormous interest in geology, palaeontology, anthropology and archaeology. Many Victorian drawing rooms had specimens from the Greensand displayed in glass-sided cabinets. They were also eagerly bought up by geology students and their professors as well as by museum curators across the country. Perhaps the best specimens can be found in the Sedgwick Earth Sciences Museum in Cambridge.

Iguanodon was a large bird-footed lizard which roamed in groups across what became East Anglia. It grew up to ten metres in length. It was probably a peaceful vegetarian with a horny beak to crop the plants and ridged cheek teeth to chew with. Its hands had a spiked thumb, possibly used in self-defence, three middle fingers and a little finger to grasp with. A broken metacarpal from the fifth digit of an iguanodon has recently been found in one of the pits on Sandy Heath, Bedfordshire. (Found by the author in Summer 1993. The bone is in his possession) It often walked on two legs to reach the leaves of trees.

The iguanodon was not the only land-based monster dug up! There was also the megalosaurus - one of the predatory theropods ("beast feet") which could grow up to nine metres. It had typical bird-like features with hollow bones, an S-shaped neck, long muscular hind legs and clawed, four-toed feet. Its lower jaw bristled with large, curved teeth. Maybe it ate iguanodon?

There were also fossils found of sea monsters too; those of the ichthyosaurus, pliosaur and plesiosaur. These were early dinosaurs which evolved from turtles. They were the first to develop openings in the skull behind their eyes. Ichthyosaurus was a sleek, dolphin-like reptile which had a long snout, sharp teeth, paddle-shaped limbs and a tall tail fin. It grew up to fifteen metres long and fed on the big swimming molluscs like the ammonites. These ammonites form the bulk of the coprolite deposit.

Another sea-going lizard found in the deposit was the barrel-bodied plesiosaurus which travelled through the water like sea-lions. It too had flippers and a deep, flattened tail and grew up to 10 metres long. A shorter-necked form of the plesiosaur was the pliosaurus. (Lambert, D. (1993), 'The Ultimate Dinosaur Book' Dorling Kindersley, pp.13,15,17,19,51, 138-9)

Fossils of another land-based dinosaur, known as Craterosaurus Pottonensis have also been reported recently. This was a relative of the stegosaurus which roamed wooded plains and browsed on low vegetation. (Seeley, H. G. (1869), 'Index Aves, Ornithosauri and Reptilia,' Catalogue, p.78; Seeley, H.G. (1874), 'On the base of a large Lacertian Cranium from the Potton Sands, presumably Dinosaurian,' Quart.Journ.Geol.Soc. vol. 40, pp.690-2; Seeley, H.G. (1912), 'Notes of British Dinosaurs, part 5 Craterosaurus,' Geol.Mag. No.6 pp.481-84; Verdcourt, B. (1988), 'Iguanodons at Potton,' Beds. Mag. vol.21 No.164 (Spring) pp.147-150) Two other monsters were found in the Greensand - the dakosaurus, a snout-nosed crocodile and the dinotosaurus. Little detail has come to light on this latter creature. (Cambridge University Library Add.7652/II.EE; Teall, (1875), pp.8-10)

Perhaps your children, nephews and nieces will know about these monsters lived in what became Cambridgeshire so many millions of years ago. There was also the more well-known crocodile found in the bed as well as a host of fossils of smaller marine and vegetable life. Many of these can be seen in the display cabinets in the Earth Science Museum on Downing Street, Cambridge.

The main value of the fossils in Victorian times was not as a record for study of prehistory but as a raw material for manure manufacturers; not just in this country but also overseas. In the late-1840s landowners were offered as little as a few shillings a ton for the coprolites. As more and more businesses joined in the rush for manures demand for coprolite rose. Royalties they paid landowners rose to between seven and fifteen shillings a ton in the early 1850s. They depended on a range of factors. The depth, extent, continuity of the seam, the angle of dip, its cleanliness, the nearness to a water source, road, wharf or station, the volume coming onto the market, knowledge or ignorance of current prices and, inevitably, nepotism - how well the contractor knew the landowner.

A new extractive industry began - an alternative and much more profitable line of work than digging clunch, clay or turf. Enid Porter, the Cambridgeshire local historian, was told that the diggers wore thick union flannel shirts, fustian trousers tied with "lalley gags", a fustian jacket with and inevitable red handkerchief. To keep the rain off their heads and the sun out of their eyes they wore a black cap with a patent leather peak. On their feet they wore fen-type boots with two or three tongues which reached four inches above the ankle. To give them a better grip in the bottom of the pit they fastened iron creepers to their boots. Iron insteps helped to prevent the boot from wearing away with the regular spade work. (Porter, E'. Notes in Cambridge Folk Museum on her conversation with C. A. Swann; Examples of the iron work can be seen in Ashwell Museum)

When the fossil seam was noticed in the Chesterton brick fields in 1848 the owners sold some of what they considered "troublesome annoyances" to Mr Deck, a chemist of Fitzroy Street, Cambridge for £2 per ton. He probably was not told the royalties the Suffolk manure manufacturers were paying but would have known that similar "phosphatic nodules" were being raised in the Felixstowe and Burwell areas. The tests he did on them showed that the Cambridgeshire "coprolites" had between 50% - 60% calcium phosphate, up to 10% higher than the Suffolk variety. It stimulated their extraction as *a matter of commercial proposition.*" (Cambridge Independent Press (CIP), 18th January, 1851, p.3)

When it was found that the seam extended to the south under Coldham's Common in Barnwell, the industry took off on a large scale. Some Suffolk manure manufacturers and entrepreneurial coprolite contractors, keen to capitalise on the demand, moved into the area to win agreements with brickyard and other landowners to raise the fossils. Gangs of experienced diggers came over to run the Cambridgeshire pits from Suffolk and other counties. (O'Connor, B. (1998), 'The Dinosaurs on Coldham's Common', Bernard O'Connor, Everton) This in-migration was not evidenced directly in the 1851 census however. There was no reference to fossil or coprolite diggers, coprolite contractors or merchants in any of the parishes where it was then being worked. It is thought that the work was just considered as labouring or, if they were employed by a farmer, as agricultural labour. Whether there were any diggings in Wicken at this time is unknown but the census showed a 12% increase over the decade to 1054. Could the additional 109 people have been a result of local diggings?

It was hardly a coincidence that the geological mapping of the country started around this time. Whilst the exploration was mainly for scientific reasons, knowledge of the extent and distribution of the Greensand was of commercial importance to those who had money to invest in what was to become known as the coprolite diggings.

The seam averaged about thirty inches (about 39cm.) thick but in places was up to six feet (2.1 metres). In some areas it was non-existent, locally called "dead land," due to a slight rise in the seabed whilst the fossils had tended to accumulate in the hollows. Yields therefore varied. In Cambridge itself it was about 300 tons per acre (0.404ha.). In one pit in Wicken it was 2,000 tons but the average was 250 tons per acre. (Kingston, A. (1889) 'Old and New Industries on the Cam.' Warren Press, Royston p.16) When annual agricultural rents were rarely over fifty shillings (£2.50) an acre and these coprolites could be sold at over £2.00 per ton, potentially several hundred pounds could be realised from an acre! Wages of agricultural labourers at that time would not have been over £25 in a year and £200 could have bought a small estate. No wonder there was a lot of interest in them. So began what has been termed by the historian, Richard Grove, as "The Cambridgeshire Coprolite Mining Rush." (Oleander Press, Cambridge, 1976)

The depth and extent of the bed had to be determined. This was done initially by digging a coffin-like pit. A cheaper method was by using a two-man corkscrew borer. Walter Tye, in his account of the Suffolk industry, included an interview with one of the diggers who said that

> "To test the depth of the coprolite he made use of a tool like a giant corkscrew, called a 'dipper,' which shuddered in his hands when striking the mineral. Local cottagers always knew what the foreman was after when he came into their gardens carrying his 'dipper.' Naturally, they strongly objected to their gardens being turned topsy-turvy, however much coprolite he might find there, and they were always delighted to see him go. Old residents today say that a sixpenny tip usually had the desired effect."
>
> (Tye, W. op.cit. p.8.)

In places the deposit was found outcropping on the surface but in most cases it had to be dug from between ten and twenty feet (3.7 – 7.4m.) of chalk marl. Where it was found on a small property it was simple matter for the landowner to take on a gang of labourers and have the fossils dug up, washed and sorted and then carted off and sold to a manure manufacturer. In this case it was commonly the farmer's own agricultural labourers. They used to dig the fossils during the low season, once the harvest was in. The work continued over the winter months and then the pits would be left to allow farm work to start in spring. In some parishes they filled with water and provided welcome swimming pools in the summer.

If the land was copyhold then the tenant might get permission to raise it using their labourers but occasionally, where a large-scale operation was envisaged, they were evicted and a coprolite manager allowed to move in to the farmhouse.

There was no security of tenure in those days. On larger properties an advertisement might be placed in the local press and tenders invited for a contractor to do the work. Farmers and others set themselves up as coprolite contractors and took on a gang of men and boys. Pick axes, crowbars, shovels, spades, planks, dog irons (supports for the planks), wheelbarrows, trucks, horses and carts, tramway rails, steam-driven pumping engines and washmills had to be bought. Wooden weatherboard sheds were needed for storing tools, engines, coal, sorting the fossils, having lunch or sheltering from the rain. All this cost money and local bank managers were keen to make loans to enterprising individuals in an industry that had such high returns.

Local traders like iron works, blacksmiths, machinists, mechanics, carpenters, carters and wheelwrights found the coprolite industry a huge boost to their trade. As did the locals brewers, beersellers and public houses landlords and landladies.,

Women and girls were employed in large numbers where the deposit was found in sandier areas. Here the fossils needed sorting to remove any unwanted stones that would reduce the quality and therefore the price paid by the manure manufacturers. As shall be seen there is considerable evidence of female employment in Wicken. The only other area of significant female employment was in Potton, near Sandy in Bedfordshire where the bed was very similar.

Contractors agreed to do the work over a set number of years with them paying the landowner a royalty of so much per ton. The tenant farmer was often compensated for the loss of revenue from those fields out of cultivation by up to £10 an acre. Once work got started the topsoil and subsoil was barrowed to one side of the field to be replaced later. In many cases it was used as the base of the washmill. As the coprolite seam was exposed the diggers shovelled it into wheelbarrows or emptied it into trucks. These were then pushed by hand or pulled by horses along a trackway or a tramway that ran out of the pit, along the hedge or drainage ditch to the edge of the field, the lode or the road to the nearest village. Here their contents were unloaded to create large piles before they were washed and sorted.

The soil above the seam on the new face was removed after undercutting, a process which caused considerable danger. Crowbars, pick-axes and shovels were used to make it collapse and, for convenience, it was just thrown into the trench already worked. As shall be seen there were numerous cases of accidents in the pits caused by collapses. This "backfilling" meant that the labourers gradually progressed across the field and onto adjoining property where a new lease was sought. Analysis of St John's College surveyors and solicitors' documents shows that sometimes pits were opened at opposite ends of the field and two gangs of diggers gradually dug their way towards each other. The washmills were also moved as the diggings progresses across the fields.

The job of washing the fossils got progressively easier over the years. Initially the technique in Suffolk was to dig a trench into the side of the estuary or the river. The actual washing and screening process was described in Walter Tye's fascinating insights into the diggings.

> "That was an old man's job when he became too old for the pit. A long tank some thirty feet in length, was specially provided for the job. The coprolites, along with a certain amount of dirt and bones, were shovelled into sieves which, when full, were placed on a ledge in the tank, just under the surface of the water; to each sieve was fastened a long pole, which the washer pulled backwards and forwards until the stones were clean. When there was a shortage of water, in or near the pit, the washing was done at the quayside before loading."

(Tye, W. op.cit. pp.3-10)

In Cambridgeshire, without access to a tidal estuary, innovative engineers used their skills to develop sophisticated washmills powered by horse or steam engine. A mound was constructed using the top and subsoil. On top of this mound a circular brick base was laid onto which a circular iron tray was placed. Large sections of the iron plates that formed the base of one such washmill have been found on Rectory Farm, Whaddon. Barrowloads of fossils were wheeled up the mound and emptied into the tray. Newcomen's invention of the steam pump led to the manufacture of many varieties and one was often installed by the works to bring the huge quantities of water needed from a nearby water source. Wells sometimes had to be dug and lined with bricks. At one time there were eleven such mills in operation in the Bassingbourn area which were claimed to have been responsible for lowing the water table of the area. (Whitaker, W. (1921), 'Water Supply of Cambs.' MGS, London, p.84. There is a photograph of a circular coprolite harrow in Cambridgeshire Collection W27.1. KO. 19554)

The working of these mills was described by the son of the Burwell doctor, Mr Lucas, whose coprolite land was the first to be exploited in Cambridgeshire. Once the coprolite had been brought to the surface

> *"The first thing to do was to throw up a hill in the middle of the ground, and this was done by first erecting- a post about ten or twelve feet long, and throwing the soil around it to a height of eleven or twelve feet and of thirty feet in diameter. Three feet from the centre a ring would be formed six to eight feet wide and four feet deep. This would be paved with bricks and the sides would be sheets of iron. On one side of the hill a platform was made from a wooden tank, to which was connected a pump eighteen feet long; a pipe from the tank would go with the ring and opposite the tank was a trapped outlet, and on the outer side of the hill a square of about two chains would be earthed up a little to*

form a sort of pan. From the central post a wooden arm would be attached about twelve to fourteen feet long; to this would be attached a wimpole tree, to which a horse would be yoked. Connected to the centre of the post would be a light rail which was fixed to the horse bridle to keep the horse always in is track; from the arm would be suspended two iron harrows which ran well in on the bottom of the ring. When the soil containing the fossils was wheeled up to the ring a sufficient quantity of water would be let in. As the horse went round a creamy fluid would be produced and the fossils would drop on the floor. Then the trapped outlet would be opened and the creamlike fluid, called "slurry" would flow into pans. This operation having been repeated a number of times the fossils on the floor would be washed clear of earth and weighed up".

(Lucas, C. (1931), 'The Fenman's World', Norwich, p.31)

The cost of constructing these mills in the late-1840s when they were first developed was £100 but by 1875 the "*coprolite contractors had become so expeditious that a hill could be put up for £5!*" (Ibid.) A description of such mills was recorded in a tourist's account of a trip in the fens.

"As we return from Burwell our eyes rest on several raised circular enclosures, round which a number of often grey horses are almost ceaselessly walking. These are the mills erected for washing the fossils. These fossils or coprolites are valuable on account of the calcic phosphate contained in them."

(Eade, David, (18--), 'Rambles in Cambridgeshire', Soham, p.48)

Another method used was similar to the vertical water wheel. Audrey Kiln's research into the industry around South Cambridgeshire included an interview with a Mr Street. He recalled the fossils being emptied into carts and taken by horse to be washed in "Hinxworth Barns".

> *"The eaves in the barn he estimated at 20 feet high. Housed in the barn was a portable steam engine, fired by wood and coal, which was connected by a belt to a huge wooden wheel which Mr Street said missed the roof by inches. Underneath the wheel was a large washing trough. The wheel had large metal cups attached to each strut. The fossils were placed into the trough and water was let in through a pipe. The wheel was driven by the engine and as the cups passed through the trough they picked up the fossils, carried them round, and replaced them in clean water at the bottom of the trough. The slurry was then released from the trough by removing a large plug. Until recent years, part of the wheel could be seen standing outside The Barn, but unfortunately there is no record of its existence now."*

(Kiln, A. (1969), 'The Coprolite Industry', Thesis for Putteridge Bury College, p.32)

In some areas a less expensive but more efficient process was developed. This was a cylindrical wash mill, rather like an early version of today's vegetable washer. They were in use over in Potton where they were described in an article in *The Bedfordshire Times.*

> *"... the coprolites are wheeled in barrows to another portion of the ground where a cylindrical sieve is fixed for the purpose of freeing them from the sand. This machine, which is worked by horse power, is a round cylinder of sheet iron, perforated with holes of a quarter inch diameter and placed horizontally in a tank of water, the cylinder being half submerged. The drum of the cylinder is two ft. in diameter at the larger end and 1 ft. at the*

smaller and 10 ft. in length.

The fossils are put in at the larger end, and as the drum revolves the smallest stones and the sand fall through the holes into the water tank, and the larger are carried along by a screw arrangement, and emptied at the smaller end into barrows. When these are filled they are wheeled by men into the sorting sheds where women are engaged in sorting. These sheds, 28 ft. long by 8 ft. wide, have on each side a bench, separated by partitions with room for one woman to work.

The fossils being largely mixed with sandstones, it is necessary that they should be removed before they are ready for market. The fossils in their mixed state, are emptied on the benches and sorted, the stones being thrown onto the floor and the fossils passed through a hole at the back of the benches into a box outside. They are then wheeled into heaps ready for sale.

(*Bedfordshire Times,* May 18th 1962. from an original article in 1878)

As the technology improved, steam powered washmills were introduced by those contractors who could afford it. After several such washings the dirty water, locally termed "slub" or "slurry" was run back into "slurry pans" to dry out before the topsoil was replaced. The theory was that once dried the cracks in it would allow better drainage. As the work progressed across the field the mill was transferred to a more accessible site. The topsoil was barrowed back into the trench or slurry pit and levelled ready for cultivation. Whilst the theory was that this process would improve the soil, in practise the operation was not always done thoroughly. It was cheaper for a contractor to cover it up quickly and move on. A farmer, however, would take care as he would benefit from improved cropping. In several areas white chalk markings can still be seen on the fields which indicate where slurry was not properly covered or the topsoil replaced. Astute land agents ensured that agreements included very precise instructions for this process and subsequent drainage, levelling and seeding.

Horses would have been a common sight hauling tumbrils loaded with washed coprolites along the lode side road to one of the docks on the River Cam. From here a barge or fenland lighter would take them up to Pope's Corner and then up the Ouse to King's Lynn for transhipment round the coast. Others may have been taken south to Cambridge where Walton's had a manure works on East Road. Some was probably carted to Burwell Big Mill which was converted to grind the coprolite as the gritstone was not hard enough. Buhrstone had to be installed in its place. (O'Connor, B. (1998), 'The Burwell Fossil Diggings', Everton)

With "super" being sold at up to £7 a ton, half the price of guano, it became much in demand across the country. It was not long therefore before sales were being promoted across Europe, in America and throughout the Empire. There were reports of sales as far afield as Russia and Queensland. (O'Connor, B. (1998) 'The Dinosaurs on Coldham's Common', Everton) During the 1850s there were four manure factories in Cambridge. With them paying an average forty-three shillings and sixpence (£2.18) a ton in 1856 for Cambridge coprolites there were profits to be made by coprolite contractors and merchants. By the 1870s the deposit was mapped in most of the Eastern Counties. Although the Upper and Lower Greensand beds were not continuous, the fossils at their base were worked in parts of Suffolk, Norfolk, Cambridgeshire, Hertfordshire, Bedfordshire, Buckinghamshire, Oxfordshire, Hampshire, Yorkshire and Kent. Its enormous extent allowed many new manure companies to capitalise on this new raw material and take a share of the increasing market for artificial fertilisers. Accordingly, many new chemical manure works were opened on the coprolite belt in Burwell, Duxford, Shepreth, Royston, Bassingbourn and Odsey. Apart from the concentration of coprolites around the lower Orwell and Deben estuaries in Suffolk, the coprolite belt extended for more that 100 miles from West Dereham in Norfolk, along the southeast fen edge through Cambridgeshire and into North Hertfordshire, Bedfordshire, Buckinghamshire and into Oxfordshire. There were isolated outcrops on the northeast coast at Speeton, near Scarborough, along the banks of the River Wey near Alton in Hampshire and near Cheriton on the southeast coast. There were also outcrops in northern and central France where they were worked extensively.

One of Cambridge's iron founders, James Ind Headley, who built the famous Eagle steam engine, was very much involved in the coprolite business. He had his own coprolite works erected behind his Eagle Foundry on Mill Road in Cambridge and had his works, "*well fitted up to make the pumps, washmills, cast iron screens and steam engines to provide power.*" (Enid Porter's notebooks Cambridge Folk Museum 15/64-65) He was aware of the investment opportunities in this area and luck had it that one of his relatives lived in Coton whose land was dug for coprolites. In the early-1850s coprolite contractors were paying landowners royalties of between seven and fifteen shillings a ton for all the coprolites they raised. This entailed having a weighbridge set up by the works and for accurate measurements to be recorded. To avoid errors and dependence on the contractors' weighings the land agents suggested an alternative scheme whereby royalties should be paid according to how many acres were dug over the year. This entailed having the pits surveyed around Lady Day (May 1st) and Michaelmas (September 29th). The surveyor's measurements could then be used to determine how much the contractor owed. This provided local companies like Bidwell, Francis, Smith, Carter Jonas and Mann and Raven a valuable additional source of income for the next forty years. Royalties ranged from as high as £400 to as low as £30 an acre but the average was about £100. This was about forty to fifty times the revenue the landowners could get from agricultural rents. After labour and other costs were deducted the contractors could make a big profit.

Throughout the 1850s the seam was worked in Cambridge and some nearby parishes. In 1854 Cambridge City Corporation gave the first licence to a Suffolk contractor, Frederick Laws. He was allowed to raise them from part of Coldham's Common. As knowledge of the local geology and the extent of the Greensand spread it became clear that it lay below many of the meadows on either side of the Cam. With the development of mass-production in the brick and tile making industry, landowners were able to bring a lot more clay land under cultivation. The rapid draining of the fens brought more land under cultivation. The digging of drainage ditches also exposed the seam and "fen tigers" - local men got involved and brought in their own gang of men and boys. They then sold it to a local manure merchant or direct to the manure manufacturers at rates that rose to over £3.00 a ton.

It was not long before the extent of the seam was traced north-eastwards along the eastern edge of the Cam as far as Wicken. The diggings in this parish centred on Wicken Fen, beneath only about ten feet (3.1m.) of cover. This was shallower than in other areas of the coprolite belt which meant lower labour costs. (Pennings and Jukes-Brown, (1881), 'Geology of the Neighbourhood of Cambridge,' Mem. Geol. Surv. London, p.34) The seam interested two geologists, Pennings and Jukes-Brown who commented that they

> "...exhibited different characters from those obtained nearer Cambridge; there was a much greater proportion of lighter coloured phosphates, and the fossils which occurred among these had not been subjected to much rolling, but retained their shells in a more perfect state than usual."

(Pennings and Jukes-Brown, 'Geology of the Neighbourhood of Cambs.,' 1881, p.38)

Those raised from pits in Fen Ditton were of a grey-black nature and may well have given rise to the term "The Ditton Treacle Mines". Workmen's clothes would have been quite a job to wash after a week in the pits.

Although there are no records of any diggings in Wicken during the 1850s that is not to say they had not started. As mentioned earlier, if the land was freehold then often the farmers employed their own labourers to do the work over the winter months. As any gangs would have conveniently avoided the census enumerator there was no direct evidence in the 1861 census. The population had actually fallen by 59 to 995. Could some of the men have moved to get work in other coprolite villages? Whilst there were alternative jobs like reed cutting for thatch, digging turf for fuel and clunch for building material, the dominant occupation was agricultural labour.

It is not known for certain who first recognised and exploited the deposit in this area of north east Cambridgeshire. It is possible that it was John Bailey Denton. a Hertfordshire surveyor. He had been instrumental in the development of the coprolite industry in and around Ashwell in Hertfordshire in the late 1850s. (Clutterbuck, Robert, (1877), 'The Coprolite Beds at Hinxworth,' *Trans. Watford Natural History Soc.* Vol. 1. p.238; Herts. CRO. 28250) Having formed his own company to raise the fossils, he went on to purchase land in Stretham. He must have been aware of the geological formation in which the fossils were found and, with relatives in this area, had become aware of the workings in Burwell.

In 1866, Denton purchased thirty acres of a field in Stretham for £600. When agricultural rents rarely went over £1.00 an acre this was an considerable sum to pay. He later went on to rent a further 39a.3r.20p in the same field at £40 per acre. Four years later he bought this latter plot for £800. Given his involvement in the coprolite industry and subsequent geological and map evidence, it seems certain that he would have exploited the underlying fossil seam. (CCRO. J.B. Denton P147/25/3; 276/T; 283/B18/21. This was field 615 on the Enclosure award map.)

This was confirmed in R. C. Reed's geological report in 1904. He stated that the seam was worked in Stretham parish from 1866 when they were found scattered in a sandy bed which lay above the Kimmeridge Clay at the foot of the Lower Greensand ridge. This ridge stretched from Haddenham, through Wilburton to Stretham where, to the east and south, the coprolites were worked along a two-mile stretch from Stretham Ferry Bridge to Stretham along the northern bank of the Ouse and on to Little Thetford. Whether Mr. Denton was involved in these workings has not been determined. Little evidence of any agreements have come to light. This is probably the result of there being such small plots of land which belonged to only small landowners whose records have not been preserved. (Reed, R.C. (1897), 'Handbook to Geology of Cambridge,' p.51; .Marr, J.E & Shipley, A.E. (1904), 'Handbook to Natural History of Cambs.',p.23; Oakley, K. (1941), 'British Phosphates', Wartime Pamphlets, Vol.8 no.3.(see fig.5))

The deposit was also found on the eastern side of the Cam valley. The first Ordnance Survey map of the area, revealed a quarry to the north of Upware from where limestone was extracted. It was used to build up the banks of the Cam. It could well have been in this excavation that the labourers found the fossils exposed in the Greensand below the Corallian Limestone. The first reference to them was in 1867 in a paper published by the geologist, Mr. J.F. Walker, of Sydney Sussex College, Cambridge. He had earlier written a paper on a discovery made in coprolite workings in Sandy, Beds., where a fascinating collection of dinosaur bones had been unearthed. Naturally his attention was drawn to this new exposure.

"On the evening before I left Cambridge I was informed by a man who brings me fossils that some new coprolite diggings had been opened in the fens. I was unfortunately unable to visit the workings then, but I have since explored them in company with Mr. Moore, of St. Catherine's College. The workings are situate about a mile from Upware, which lies about twelve miles from Cambridge, and seven from Ely.

Upware is known to geologists as the nearest locality of the Coralline Oolite to Cambridge. The bed differs from the "Sandy conglomerate bed," in being less ferruginous and containing more lime, probably derived from the Coralline Oolite. The nodules are mixed with pebbles which are picked out by women and children; about a third part is waste. Roller washers are used here as at Sandy. The sections exposed by the workings differ considerably; the best I have seen was on the occasion of my last visit to the pits.

Surface, black peaty soil, often containing bones of red deer, horse etc.	*1ft.6in.*
Layer of light- coloured Coprolites	*1 0*
Sand (called by the workmen silt)	*1 6*
Vein of dark-coloured Coprolites	*0 9*
Silt	*1 6*
Vein of Dark-Coprolites	*1 0*
Clay (not pierced)	

At another working -	
Sand	*6ft.0ins*
Coprolitic vein	*2 0*
Conglomerate (hard rock)	*0 4*
Light-coloured sand and clay	

(Walker, J.F. (1867), 'On Some New Coprolite Workings in the Fens,' Geol.Mag.v.p.309)

Unfortunately, he gave no indication whether it was a contractor working these pits or a local farmer who had taken advantage of the discovery to realise the vast profits to be made. According to Henry Keeping, another geologist, these particular workings were discontinued by 1868. Their lower phosphate compared to other Cambridgeshire workings, made them less economic. (Keeping, H. (1868) 'Discovery of Gault with Phosphatic stratum at Upware' *Geol. Mag.* vol.v. pp.272-3)

However, better quality and more easily extracted deposits were found in close proximity in Fodder Fen. Some pits were up to fifteen feet (4.6m.) deep. Over the next three years the greater part of this Fen, the shelving ground to the west of the low Corallian Limestone Ridge, was worked. A series of cuts were dug towards the Cam and in one pit, where two seams coalesced to form a single bed 2ft. 6" (0.76m.) thick, there was a very high yield. When average yields were about 250 tons per acre and, at its peak, the manure manufacturers were paying over £3.00 per ton for the coprolites, one can see why it attracted so much interest. But few people are aware of its existence today.

Fodder Fen Drove track would have been busy with local families out walking to work and back and many horses and carts would have been in evidence hauling the fossils to the riverside. Here they would have been unloaded onto barges or the fenland lighters and then transported to the manure works. Thomas Thwaites Ball, of Burwell, who first attracted the Ipswich manure manufacturer, William Colchester, to the deposit in his fields, used a local windmill to grind the fossils. By 1865 they had gone into business together and erected a chemical manure works on the banks of Burwell Lode. They bought many of the local fossils to be processed at their works. Unfortunately, none of the documentary evidence from this business shows which local farmers or landowners were supplying them with coprolites. However, it was possible that a Mr. Schofield acted as a middle man buying them from farmers and then arranging their sale to manure manufacturers.

In early summer 1870 one of the local newspapers, the *Cambridge Independent Press*, reported two events at the coprolite works. They were referred to as in Wicken but it is not certain that the diggings had extended to this parish by then. It seems more than likely they were referring to the workings at Upware. However, subsequent evidence shows that a shallow seam was found in similar locations on the eastern slopes of Fen Side, the low ridge that runs north-northwest out of the parish. It was here perhaps where the following incidents were reported.

*"**WICKEN**. Accident at Coprolite Works. On Tuesday morning last a labourer named John Bailey, had his legs severely bruised by a large quantity of earth falling on him at the coprolite works."*

(*Cambridge Independent Press*, 21st May 1870 p.8)

*"**WICKEN**. Discovery of Skeleton. -On Saturday, 21st May, there was discovered at the coprolite works about two feet from the surface, a male skeleton; most of the bones were perfect. The head was taken care of but the remaining portion of the bones were collected and buried again."*

(*Cambridge Independent Press*, 4th June 1870 p.8)

The same summer Charles Bidwell, a surveyor based in Ely, reported that Thomas Thwaites Ball had an agreement with a landowner at Wicken. Who it was was not stated. As mentioned earlier, Ball was already involved in the business in Burwell. His gang of workmen had finished operations and he wanted to expand into Holt Fen, in Thetford. He contacted the owner, Charlotte Yarrow, requesting a lease for two further acres.

"I rather want to commence at Stretham as I have one of my Wicken Foremen now ready to take charge and he will be leaving me unless I keep him on somewhere. It will take the men 2 or 3 weeks to get the washing mill up and the shed erected. I therefore wish you would take the first instalment (£70) and allow me to commence raising Mill etc."

(CCRO. 283/B13/25)

Ball was probably not the only outside contractor involved. It is quite possible that local farmers who owned small plots of coprolite land would have arranged, like Mrs. Yarrow, to have the fossils raised. It is most likely that they employed their own farm labourers rather than having a coprolite contractor move in.

Where the seam was found over a larger area the land agents recommended that the landowner invite tenders. Depending on the offers an outside contractor, like Mr. Ball, would have taken on the work. In the early-1840s - 1850s royalties of between four and fifteen shillings (£0.20 - £0.75) a ton were paid but by the 1860s it was more common for royalties per acre. These averaged £100 but ranged from as little as £20 an acre up to £200.

A large amount of capital was needed to purchase the necessary plant and machinery to manage the site. This included spades, shovels, crowbars, planks, dog irons (supports for planks across the trench), carts, wheelbarrows, sheds, horses, steam engines, sieves and washmills. As a result there was scope for entrepreneurs to capitalise on the work. Foremen would have been taken on and gangs of men, women, girls and boys hired. These were not necessarily local people as the foreman, as in Mr. Ball's case, would often come from nearby workings and bring his own gang. This occasionally led to confrontations and there is every likelihood the local "fen tigers" were involved in this kind of gang labour. Work gangs were common in the fens and, although little has emerged of the social impact of the coprolite diggings in this area, there were cases of unrest in the village. Many farmers across Cambridgeshire and the fens experienced outbreaks of incendiarism from disaffected labourers. Low wages, poor treatment and lack of job security were often the causes. Whether it was because outside labourers were taken on at higher pay instead of them is not known.

In the early days of the diggings the technology was fairly basic. The topsoil was barrowed to one side of the field to be stored for replacement when the work was finished. Where a washmill was to be sited a mound of the topsoil, 9.2m wide and 3.7m high was built up and a circular ring of bricks was laid on top. The fossils were then emptied into a circular iron trough that lay on the bricks. Where there was no surface drainage on the site a well was often sunk or a horse-drawn water barrel was used. A horse dragged an iron harrow around the inside of the tank to clean the sand and earth from the stones. Later, if the contractor could afford it, a steam-powered cylindrical washer was used, similar to the present day vegetable washer. This was referred to in Walker's 1866 article. The dirty water, slurry or slub was released from the tank and, in theory, allowed to dry out before the topsoil was replaced. The resultant cracking would facilitate drainage. Human nature meant that not all work went according to plan and many patches of subsoil on the surface are the result of the job not having been done properly. The fossils were taken to sheds to be sorted. Mobile sheds were used which could be taken into the next field as the trenches progressed. Unwanted pebbles were removed and the coprolites stored in heaps ready for transport. Horse and cart was the most common form of transport but, if the contractor could afford it, a steam engine hauled trucks along a tramway down to the nearest riverbank or railway siding.

Near Streatham there is actually a ramp up to the embankment by the river which may well have been erected by the men to allow the carts or barrows to empty the fossils into the barges or shallow draught fen lighters. These had brought down coal, hops and other goods from King's Lynn and went back loaded with coprolites. A John Denton, possibly a relative of Bailey Denton, was Toll Keeper on the river at this time. The increased traffic occasioned by the coprolite trade allowed the river transport system to continue well into the 1880s. (Cambs.R.O.P147/25/3; 276/T; 283/B18/21)

On the 26th January 1871 John and Henry Hall of Ely, allowed Charles Roads, a coprolite merchant from Meldreth, Cambridgeshire, to raise the coprolite from 14a.0r.33p. of Hall Fen in Stretham. Roads compensated the yearly tenant, William Drever, for the loss of his land due to the diggings. The Halls received a royalty of £100 per acre and Roads agreed to work up to 4.6m at two and a half acres a year for four years. He also was allowed to take advantage of any gravel he raised, paying £0.04 for every cubic yard. (Cambs.R.O.515/B Henry Hurrell's Madingley papers) By the end of the summer that year the seam had been discovered further north as on 29th September an Ely farmer,

Henry Hazell, allowed Charles Darwson, a merchant from Little Shelford, near Cambridge, a licence to raise all the coprolites under seven acres of Smith's Fen. He must have been particularly keen to work the deposit as the agreement stipulated that he only work one acre a year. He was given permission to erect a washmill, to sink a well and to lay a tramway. The royalty was £30 less than those being paid in Stretham and Upware so he must have been keen to realise a good profit from the operation. (Camb.R.O.283B13/28)

Apart from Messrs. Ball and Roads there was also Schofield and Co. They advertised in the Post Office Directory as coprolite merchants and evidence shows they sold £188 of Wicken coprolites to the Farmers Manure Company in Royston between 1870-1. The company records confirmed that the local fossils were of poorer quality than other Cambridgeshire coprolites. "Whole" Wicken coprolites sold at £2.00 per ton in 1871. They dropped to £1.90 per ton in 1872 compared to £2.50 for Cambridgeshire coprolites. "Ground" Wicken coprolites sold at £2.50, £0.50 less than their rivals. (Herts. RO.D/Eky.B1)

Despite their lower value the quantities available meant there was an enormous amount of labour required. The 1871 census showed that Wicken, like many other "coprolite villages," had experienced a dramatic population increase since 1861. This was attributed "to extensive coprolite digging having attracted numbers of labour". In fact, numbers had risen by 138 since 1861, a dramatic reversal in the trend. It was also able to boast of having the largest number of coprolite workers in 1871 in any of the parishes on the entire coprolite belt; 181 people out of a village population of 1133. This meant that just over one in every six living in the parish was involved. An analysis of the census returns reveals remarkable insight into the social structure of the industry.

The only farmer mentioned as being involved was Layton Slack of Fenside who, back in 1861 also acted as a Methodist preacher. By 1871 it seemed he had forgone this role as he described himself only as a farmer of 167 acres "employing 12 men and 4 boys, also employing 11 men and 4 boys coprolite digging and 14 women as pickers." Other farmers would probably got their labourers to raise the fossils but, apart from Mr. Slack, no evidence has come to light. It is possible that they arranged for a contractor, like Ball, to work them as they had the available capital to invest in the spades, shovels, barrows, planks, horses, washmills, engines, pumps, sieves, wells, washmills and tramways etc. needed on site.

The other 151 coprolite labourers and coprolite pickers worked as part of "private gangs". There was no evidence of any foremen or women so there may not have been the hierarchy that the male dominated groups had in other coprolite parishes. Wicken actually had by far the most number of women and girls employed in any coprolite village, 84 in fact. They were only employed in areas where there was a large proportion of gravels and unwanted stones in the deposit. Their job was to pick and sort the fossils before they were sent off to the manure manufacturers. This would have given them a better income than agricultural labour and, for many, gave them financial independence. Other villages where there was a female element in the workforce were Potton and Sandy, Beds where the deposit was similarly found on the Lower Greensand.

There is plenty of evidence of the work being very much a family affair. There were numerous cases of husbands and wives working together and also of parents and children. 28-year old Simon Bishop worked with his wife Ann, 27, two daughters, 10 and 7 and an 8 year old son. 46-year old Hockley Bishop worked with his wife Susan, 46, and four children. 50-year old Joseph Rumblelow worked with his four children and his sister. Many young sisters worked together, presumably with friends and neighbours, which would have helped relieve the boredom of the sorting sheds. (See author's account of Potton for more evidence of women's involvement and the sorting sheds)

Age	Male	Female
0 - 6	0	0
7 - 13	22	20
14 - 18	24	27
19 - 25	20	21
26 - 40	23	14
Over 40	7	3
Total	96	85
Average age	21.6	20.0
Eldest	54	49
Youngest	8	7
% born locally	98.0	94.3

(Cambs.R.O. 1871 census)

The table above, abstracted from the 1871 census, reveals an interesting pattern in the age structure of those employed in Wicken parish. Whilst it was almost equally balanced in term of sex, the bulk were young children. Forty-two were aged under 14. This was despite the introduction of the 1870 Education Act whose aim was to provide education for these very groups. Although there was slightly more teenage boys employed, there were relatively similar numbers in those groups up to forty. As the average age was only 21 for men and 20 for women one cannot help envisaging a number of romances developing amongst them. Perhaps, given Slack's religious inclinations, the men were better behaved than some all-male gangs in other parts of the coprolite belt. There were many cases of drunkenness, theft, assault etc. The fact that it was almost totally local people involved must have helped make it very much a community effort. This must similarly have had a beneficial influence on village life.

In Stretham eight people described themselves as being involved, very few, given the circumstances. There were six men as diggers and two young girls aged 12 and 15 as pickers, whereas in Little Thetford there were twenty involved. These included a 30-year old woman and two girls of 12 and 13. The men's average age was 22 but ranged from 52 to a ten year old

Lower Cretaceous Terrestrial Communities
a *Iguanadon* (Vertebrata: Reptilia: Archosaur – dinosaur)
b *Megalosaurus* (Vertebrata: Reptilia: Archosaur – dinosaur)
c *Hypsilophodon* (Vertebrata: Reptilia: Archosaur – dinosaur)
d *Acanthopholis* (Vertebrata: Reptilia: Archosaur – dinosaur)
e *Equisetites* (Pteridophyta: Calamites – horsetails)

(McKerrow, W.S.. (1978), *The Ecology of Fossils: An Illustrated Guide,*
Duckworth, p.297)

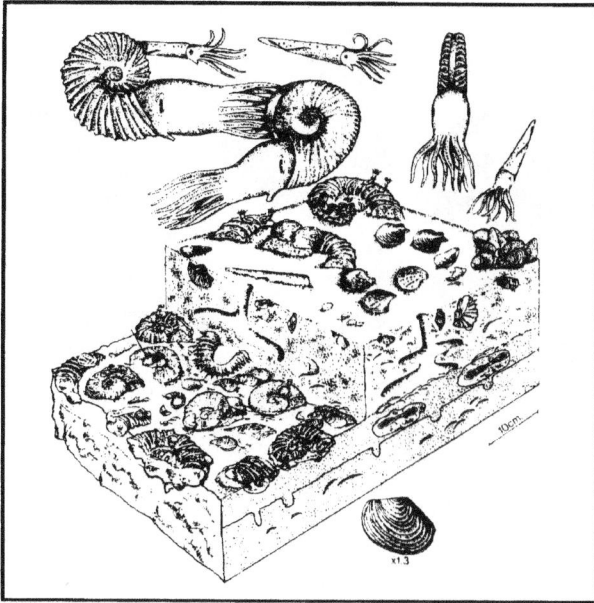

The Phosphate bed Community
(McKerrow, W.S.. (1978), *The Ecology of Fossils: An Illustrated Guide,*
Duckworth, p.286)

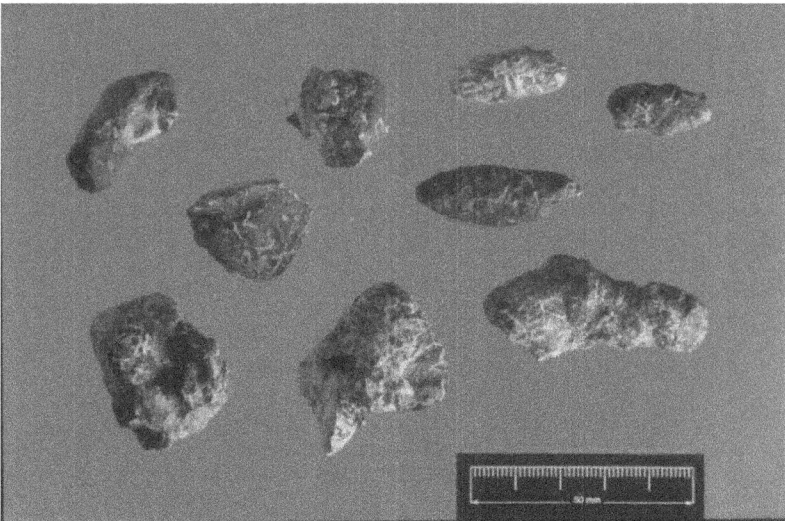

Cambridgeshire coprolites. (Photograph courtesy of Earth
Sciences Museum, Cambridge)

Cambridgeshire coprolites, thought to be 170 million
years old. (Courtesy of Tim Gane)

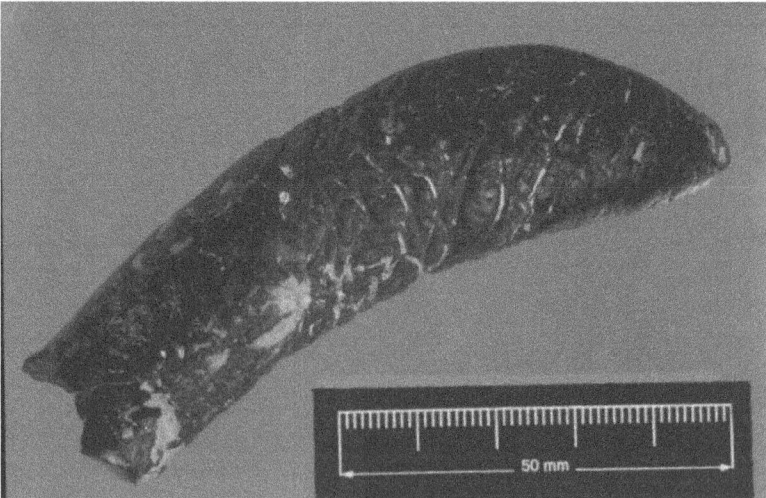

The Barrington coprolite
(Photograph courtesy of Earth Sciences Museum, Cambridge)

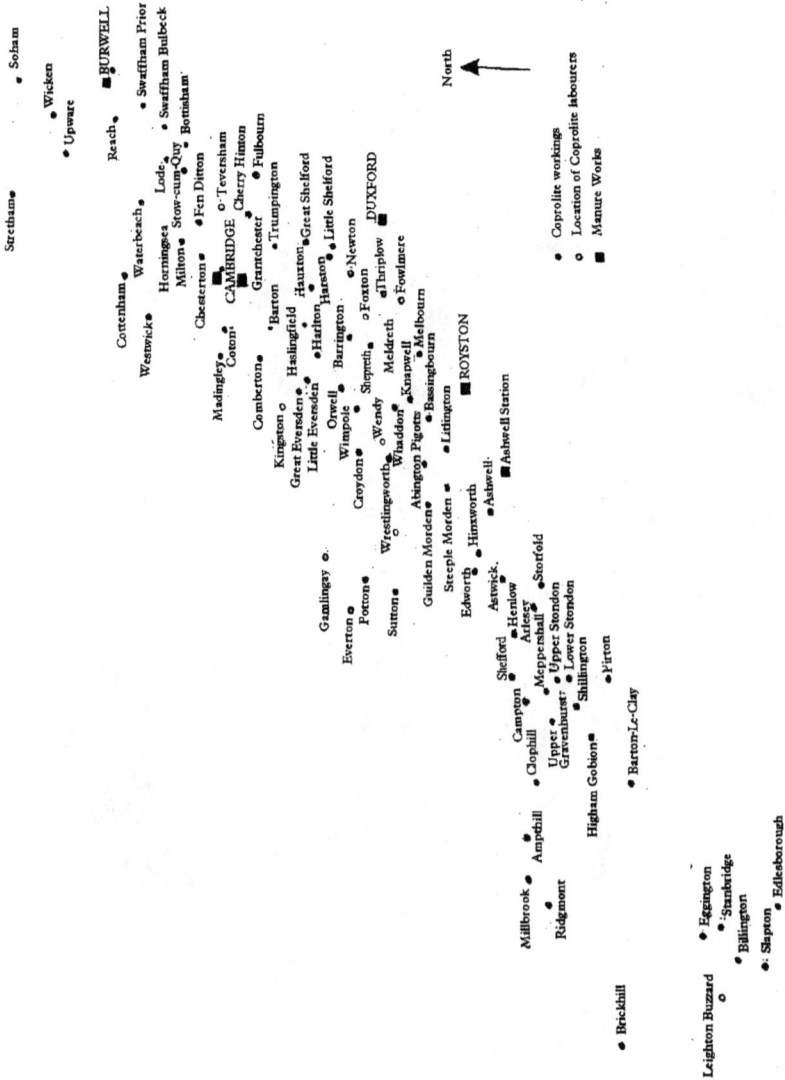

North ←

Legend:
- • Coprolite workings
- o Location of Coprolite labourers
- ■ Manure Works

Place names shown on the map:

Stretham, Soham, Wicken, Upware, BURWELL, Reach, Swaffham Prior, Swaffham Bulbeck, Bottisham, Cottenham, Waterbeach, Horningsea, Lode, Stow-cum-Quy, Milton, Fen Ditton, Teversham, Cherry Hinton, Fulbourn, Westwick, Chesterton, Coton, CAMBRIDGE, Grantchester, Trumpington, Barton, Haslingfield, Hauxton, Harlton, Hauxton, Great Shelford, Little Shelford, Newton, Thriplow, DUXFORD, Fowlmere, Madingley, Comberton, Kingston, Great Eversden, Little Eversden, Orwell, Barrington, Foxton, Wimpole, Wendy, Stepeth, Meldreth, Knapwell, Croydon, Wrestlingworth, Whaddon, Abington Pigots, Bassingbourn, Melbourn, Litlington, ROYSTON, Ashwell, Himsworth, Guilden Morden, Steeple Morden, Ashwell Station, Gamlingay, Everton, Potton, Sutton, Edworth, Astwick, Henlow, Stotfold, Shefford, Arlesey, Campton, Meppershall, Upper Stondon, Lower Stondon, Clophill, Upper Gravenhurst, Shillington, Pirton, Higham Gobion, Barton-Le-Clay, Millbrook, Ampthill, Ridgmont, Brickhill, Leighton Buzzard, Eggington, Stanbridge, Billington, Slapton, Edlesborough, Dinton, Bishopstone, Ford

Coprolite Diggings at Orwell, Cambridgeshire. 1860s – 1870s
(Courtesy of Cambridgeshire Collection W27.1J80 25358)

Coprolite Diggings in Cow Pasture, Abington Pigotts, Cambridgeshire, 1883
(Courtesy of Mr and Mrs Sclater, Abington Pigotts)

Photographs of the coprolite works on Sandy Heath, Bedfordshire, c.1882) The top photo shows women outside the sorting shed. The lower photographs shows a horse-powered cylindrical washmill. (Courtesy of Potton History Society)

Undated photograph of windmills in Bassingbourn, which, once the harvest had been milled, the millstones were replaced with buhr-stones to grind the coprolites. Horse-drawn carts brought the copro-lites along the road from diggings in nearby parishes.

Undated postcard of Bird's manure factory at Duxford, which was used to grind local coprolites and produce superphosphate.

Steam engine hauling coprolites from Whaddon to Shepreth Station c.1880
(Cambridge Collection Q AR J8 11029 Courtesy of Mrs Coningsby, Whaddon

Undated postcard of horse-drawn tumbrils carrying coprolites to the railway station at Millbrook, Bedfordshire.

HORSE-POWERED COPROLITE WASHMILL

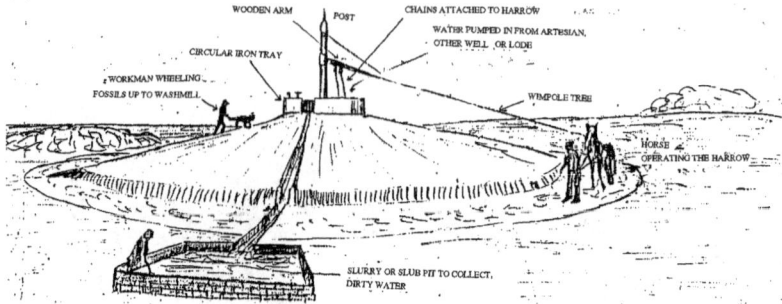

(Based on sketch in Richard Grove's Cambridgeshire Coprolite Mining Rush)

Undated photograph of a circular coprolite harrow
Cambridgeshire Collection: W27.1. KO. 19554).

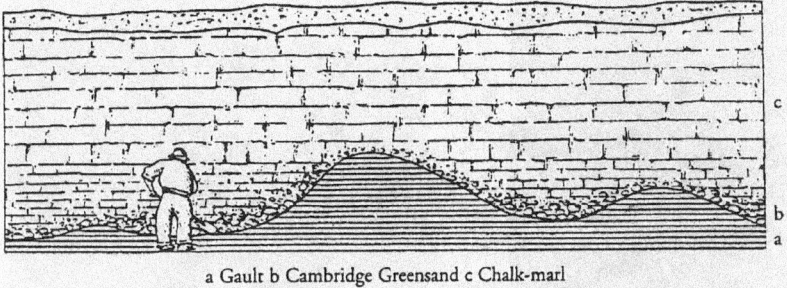

a Gault b Cambridge Greensand c Chalk-marl

View of a coprolite pit in Horningsea, Cambs.
(Jukes-Browne, A.J. & Hill, W. *Cretaceous Rocks of Britain,* Mem. Geol. Surv. 1903, p.194)

Undated photograph of coprolite diggers in Orwell, Cambridgeshire
(Courtesy of Sue Miller, Orwell History Society)

Photographs of the coprolite works on Sandy Heath, Bedfordshire, c.1882) The top photo shows women outside the sorting shed. The lower photographs shows a horse-powered cylindrical washmill. (Courtesy of Potton History Society)

Caricature of J.B. Lawes who patented the technique of dissolving coprolite and other phosphatic materials in sulphuric acid to produce superphosphate. He set up his own manure company, won contracts to raise coprolites and purchased others from diggings across south-east England (*Vanity Fair* 8th July 1882)

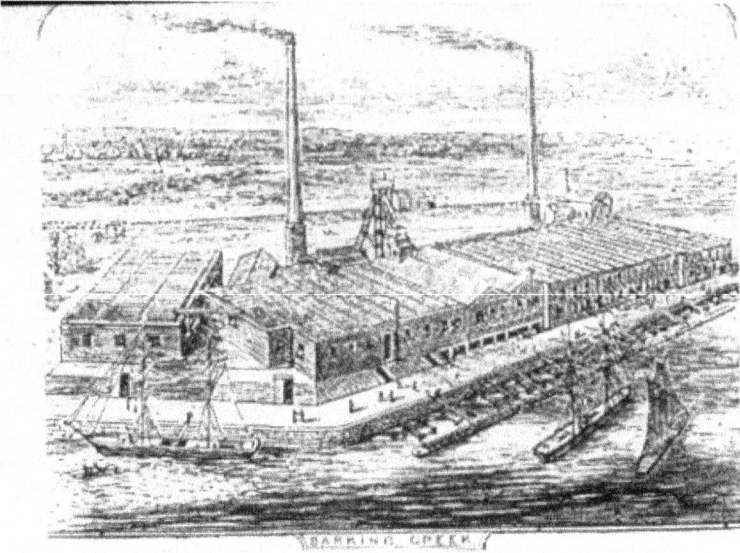

LAWES' MANURE FACTORY, DEPTFORD CREEK.

(Courtesy of Lawes Agricultural Trust, Rothamsted Agricultural Station)

Undated photograph of coprolites being unloaded at Lawes'
Chemical Manure Works at Barking, London
(Courtesy of Rural History Centre, Reading University Neg. No.
35/23594)

R. & H. WALTON,

MANUFACTURERS OF ALL KINDS OF

MANURES,

EAST ROAD, AND COLDHAM ROAD,

CAMBRIDGE.

Blood Manure, Corn Manure, Turnip Manure, Mangold Manure,
SUPERPHOSPHATE OF LIME,
PREPARED NIGHT SOIL FOR CORN.

The following articles supplied in any quantity for mixing purposes:—
Half Inch Bones; Quarter Inch Bones; Sulphuric Acid;
Muriatic Acid; Sulphate of Ammonia; Agricultural Salt;
Soot; &c., &c.

Experienced Men sent out for mixing if required.

BONE AND MANURE WORKS,

EAST ROAD, AND COLDHAM ROAD, CAMBRIDGE.

Robert Walton's advert, Kelly's Post Office Directory 1864

Undated photograph of Edward Packard (1819 – 1899) who
founded Edward Packard and Company. In 1843 he began making superphosphate by dissolving old bones in sulphuric acid at Snape Mill. In
1851 he built Britain's first complete sulphuric acid and superphosphate
works at Bramford and went on to win coprolite agreements and purchase coprolites from across southeast England.
(http://www.yara.com/en/about/yara_centennial/heritage/
fisons_inter.html)

1861 photograph of William Colchester (1813–1898), one of the first manure manufacturers to use Suffolk coprolites. Had manure works in Ipswich, moved into Cambridgeshire fens in 1846, won coprolite contracts and purchased others from diggings across southeast England.
(Courtesy of Giles Colchester)

The extent of the coprolite diggings across Cambridgeshire
(Grove, R. (1976), The Cambridgeshire Coprolite Mining Rush,
Oleander Press)

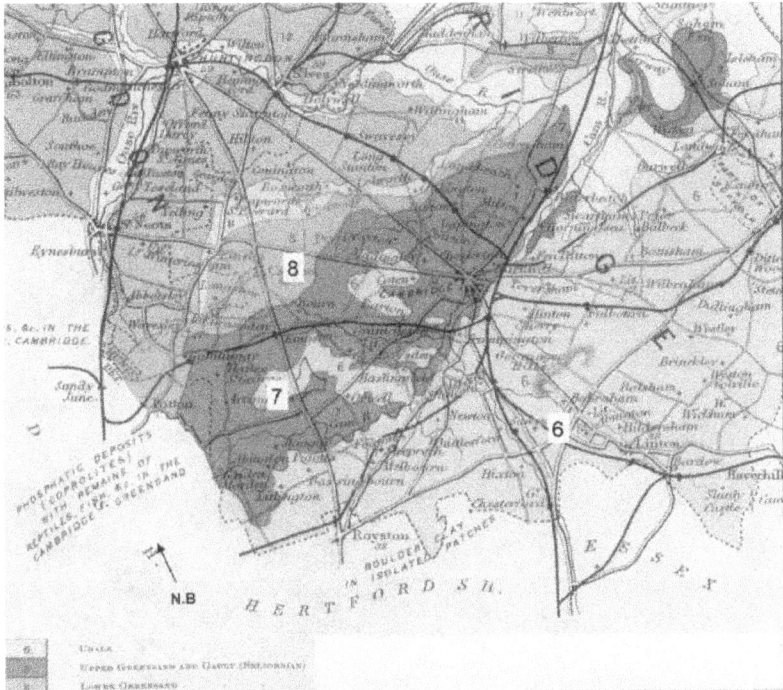

Extract from geological map of south-west Cambridgeshire after
Woodward (1904 based on Reynolds (Ian West 2001)
6 = Chalk; 7 = Upper Greensand; 8 = Lower Greensand

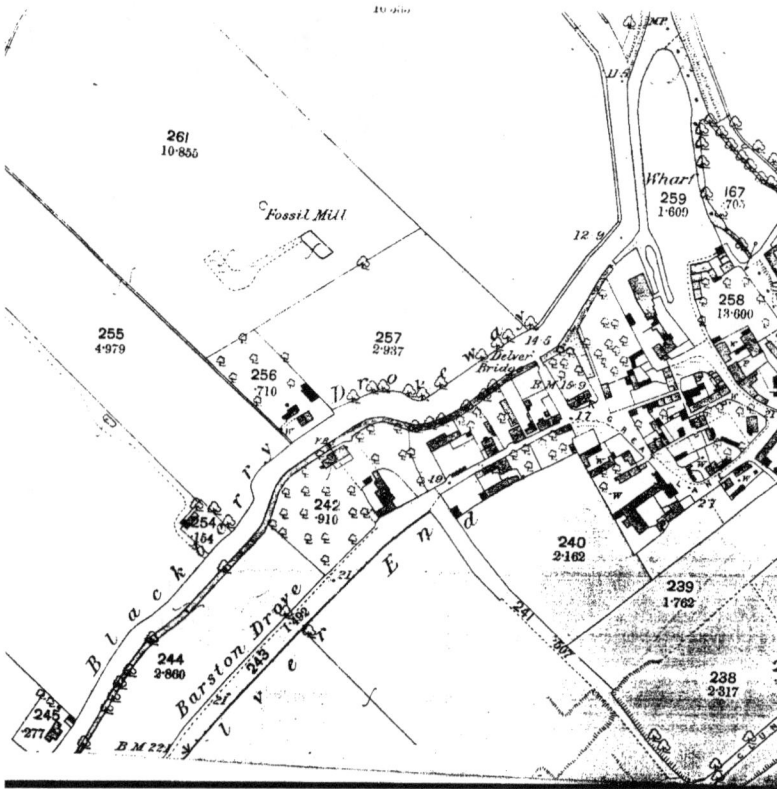

No map evidence of the diggings on Wicken Fen has come to light. This map shows one of the fossil mills near Reach. (1st edition 25-inch maps, Cambs.)

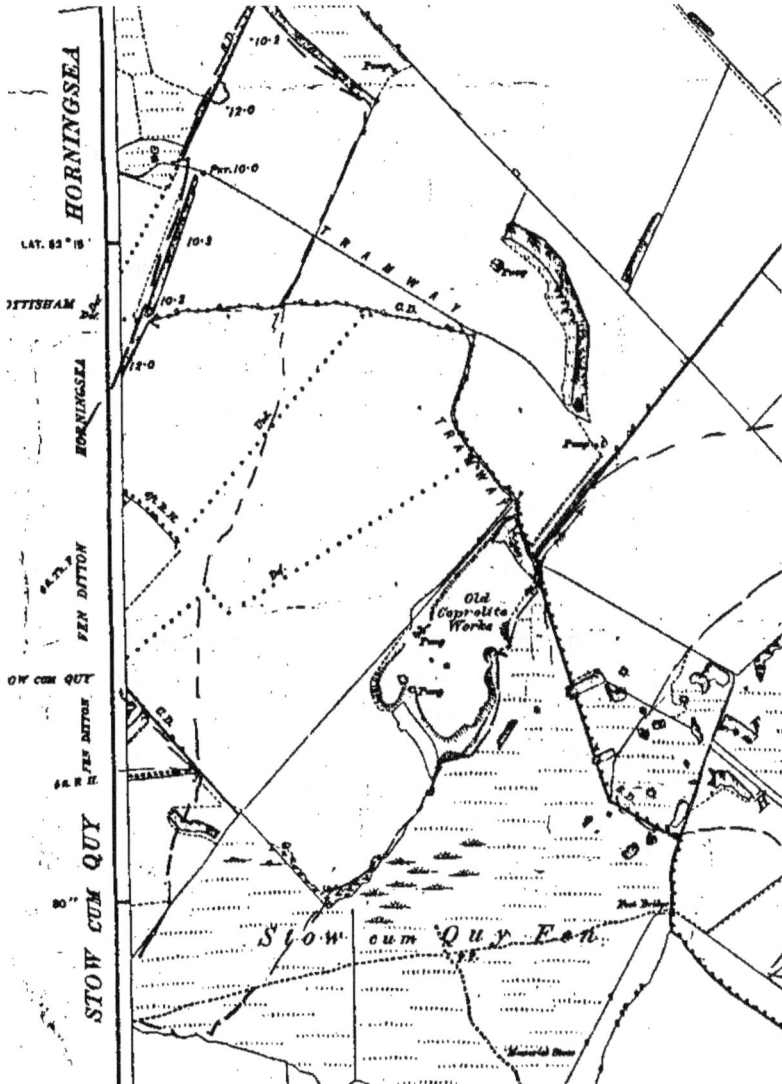

Extract from 1st Edition OS map showing Quy Fen
coprolite works, water-filled trenches, old washmill
sites and the tramway to the River Cam at Clayhythe

and two nine year olds and boy. As 70% were born in the parish and 20% came from other Cambridgeshire parishes it was predominantly work for the locals.

There was only one man from Wilburton, probably walking down to work in the pits by the river. Only four actually lived in Stretham village proper; the rest lived outside or near Thetford or on the other side of the river. The historian, Derek Plumb, in his account of the industry in Stretham, commented that it had a short-term but significant impact on the local economy. He gave no references to actual workings in the parish. Over the twenty or so years the fossils were worked, the extra income generated for farmers and labourers alike would have been a very welcome addition, as would the trade it generated in subsidiary industries.

" Some 21 families had links with coprolite, but of the 28 persons employed by the mines, 22 were younger members of family groups, or indeed servants of, or lodgers in, those households. The fact that the majority of the heads of the households kept their previous employment, that they were not lured into taking up work in the new industry is important and shows a marked contrast to employment patterns on the railway."

	Ages	Stretham	Thetford
Males	9 - 13	0	4
	14 - 18	1	2
	19 - 24	2	7
	25 - 30	2	3
	Over 30	1	1
Females	9 - 13	1	2
	14 - 18	1	0
	25 - 30	0	1
Total		8	20
% of workers		1.5	16.2
% of total population		0.8	6.0

(Plumb, Derek J., 'The Parish of Stretham 1840-1890', Cambridge Collection)

Clearly, Thetford employed considerably more at that time which suggests the workings had progressed northwards along the river towards the village.

The number of children employed was a matter of concern. Child abuse was reported amongst fenland gangs. Exploitation with low wages and poor working conditions was common in factories, on farms and in domestic labour. A Parliamentary Commission was set up to investigate. It shed light on the situation in this area when Rev. C.W. Franchen, the Wicken vicar, in his 1867 report to the Commission, gave some details about the age structure of one gang of sixty-five children!

Age	Males	Females
Under 7	0	0
Between 7 and 13	25	15
Between 13 and 18	10	15

"Private gangs little known in Cambs. except in a few parishes where children are employed gathering coprolites, an employment hardly coming under the category of agricultural labour... The sexes work apart. The overseers in this parish are generally moral and religious characters and have wholesome influence on the conduct of the children. Otherwise the consequences are baneful and dreaded by the parents."

(Parliamentary Papers 1867-8 XVII "1st Report of the Commissioners on the Employment of Children, Young Persons and others in Agriculture'.

Light was shed on the "baneful" conditions in other parishes. The social life of the diggers led Samuel Hopkins, the village grocer, postmaster and the deacon to the Bassingbourn Congregational Church reported how

"...the discovery of coprolites... brought together a large influx of persons from all parts who were employed in digging them out of the earth. These persons were the refuse of society, and with few exceptions, were extravagant, intemperate, licentious, depraved and atheistical in their conduct. One of the principal employers was an avowed Infidel. By his example, by his distribution of pernicious writings and tracts, the minds of many became infected.

The employment of these men (who are called Diggers) was lucrative. They earned much money, they required lodgings. Consequently they were spread all over the village and neighbourhood. Whenever they lodged, with a few exceptions, they caused a spiritual blight, the people became indifferent, careless in their attendances and unconcerned about their state; many who were hopeful characters fell away and gave evidence that an increase in riches is destructive of spiritual life.

To meet this gigantic evil, fresh evangelistic efforts were put forth, with the aid of surrounding friends, a large room was built for the use of these people for reading and instruction on week days and for divine service on the Sunday evenings, an evangelist was also employed to converse with them, or preach, distribute tracts and endeavour to restrain them, but drunkenness and immorality so awfully and universally prevailed that these efforts for their salvation were fruitless. Some of these characters would occasionally attend our services, one or two were brought under the power of the word and were added to the church.

To prevent the spread of infidelity Mr. Harrison gave lecture series with the assistance of other visiting ministers. The increase of population by the opening of the coprolite pits and the widespread wickedness caused thereby made his position more trying than any of his predecessors experienced yet he ceased not to warn the wicked."

(Hopkins, Samuel, Original MS in possession of Deacon of Bassingbourn Congregational Church, pp.210ff., Xerox copies in Cambs. Collection and CUL)

The Commissioners were also provided with a report from a school teacher who was employed at the MP, Arthur Peel's coprolite works on Sandy Heath, Beds.

SANDY 50. Mr. Coulson. - "Girls of 7 years up to 18 years are employed in the coprolite works. The work is taken by the piece; they get a sum per ton for picking over the fossils. A girl of ten years would earn 7s. a week by day work, but much more by piece work. The state of education among them is very low; some can read, hardly any can write. The parents also are very uneducated. This and the adjoining district of Polton (sic) is a gardening tract; children are much employed in large numbers in peeling onions and such like work. I have seen gross cases of immorality and indecency, even among the smaller children, at leisure moments at the coprolite mills when waiting for the carts, and have heard much bad language, which is readily learnt by the young from constantly hearing it round them. The foremen do not check them. The sexes should be separated at the mills, by means of different sheds, or even by separate mills for boys and girls. In one instance the foreman keeps a public house, where the wages are paid, and the men and children are allowed to have as much drink as they like during the week on credit, and the money is deducted on pay night. These children have no time for learning, except in the evening."

(Parliamentary Papers 1867-8 XVII "1st Report of the Commissioners on the Employment of Children, Young Persons and others in Agriculture'. pp.108, 343, 506, 518.Evidence to Mr. Portman and his Summary.)

Whilst this took place about fifty miles away, one can imagine it could similarly have been the case in Upware and Wicken.

The following table shows that the diggings did not completely dominate Wicken's employment. Farming still maintained its control over the area but the diggings were clearly a very significant secondary activity that must have helped to expand the local economy during the years that they were in operation.

Farmers and Sons	34
Agricultural Labourers	204
Other Male occupations	65
Male Coprolite labourers	95
Female Coprolite Labourers	85

(Cambs.R.O. 1871 census returns)

It was earlier mentioned that Layton Slack lived on Fenside but three other farmers who lived in the same area did not report to the census enumerator that they were employing coprolite labourers. Most of those employed in the diggings lived on Front Street and Lower Drove with a few living at Gunner Hall (sic) and Thorn Hall. One local inn, with the sign, *"Five miles from Anywhere. No Hurry,"* was the centre of Upware. It would have been well frequented by the diggers. According to the 1871 census, William Cousin was the publican and there were four coprolite labourers lodging there. In fact, many inns and beerhouses were opened specifically for the diggers, serving breakfast before the men went to work and, like this pub, providing warmth in the evenings, an evening meal, beer, company and overnight lodgings.

Between 1871 and 1873 there must have been a renewed and greater demand for local phosphates. Geological reports showed that three further pits were opened in Upware to the north of original pit. Here the seam was found to dip northwards at an angle of five degrees that would have incurred somewhat greater labour costs in their extraction. However, this would have been compensated given the higher yields.

In 1872, the Ely surveyor, Charles Bidwell, reported on the allotment belonging to the late Mrs. Mary Slack in Fodder Fen. 17a.1r.4p. had been dug and the work was still continuing. (Cambs.R.O. Bidwell 28 p.168 marked as field numbers 212,251,252,253 on the enclosure map) Further documentation indicated another coprolite contractor, Henry Wilkerson, of Eversden near Cambridge had become involved. He had earlier been in financial difficulties with St. John's College over coprolite workings in Ashwell and by April 1873, had almost finished in Fodder Fen.

Henry Fordham, the Ashwell landowner, coprolite contractor and a director of the Farmers Manure Company, went with him to the auction of *"Coprolite Plant comprising 1000 yards of wrought iron tramway as laid, now in use at Mr. Wilkerson's Works next the river Cam."* It realised £206.37 with half the cost accounted for by the tramway. Mr. Nunn, the chairman of the Manure Company, bought the bulk. These would have then been sent by train and carts to Nunn's own coprolite works on his Bassingbourn Farm whilst most of the actual plant was sold to Mr. Slack. He must still have been working his own coprolites. Mr. Dennis, a local landowner, bought some of the plant. Details of the sale were available from his foreman and also from the Inn. (Cambs.R.O. 296/B929.1; CUL. Royston Crow, 4th April, 1873)

In 1874 Bidwell gave a talk on coprolites to the Institute of Surveyors. He had been surveying the coprolite workings across Cambridgeshire since the 1860s and referred to local workings in his speech.

> *"The coprolite pits which have been opened at Wicken in Cambridgeshire, close to the banks of the Cam, are very remarkable, the vein being within about four feet of the surface, and of enormous thickness and extent, yielding at least 2000 tons to the acre; but the fossils are not of so great a quality as the Cambridge stones. They contain only about 20 to 30 percent of superphosphate, and are of a browner colour and smoother texture than the Cambridge fossil, and are also very much intermixed with gravel and pebbles, so that they require to be hand picked by women and children, - a very expensive process. These coprolites are worth in the market about 25s. to 30s. per ton. The Soham, Thetford and Stretham coprolites are also of this class; but they are not found in such great quantities. Their value never exceeds £100 per acre, and rarely reaches it."*

(Bidwell, C. (1874), 'On Coprolites', Trans.Inst.Surv.pp.305-6)

The early 1870s was a period of economic boom with investment in most sections of industry. The large demand for coprolite labour actually has been acknowledged as having an inflationary effect on the local agricultural economy. Apart from the decline in farm labour occasioned by the gradual introduction of farm machinery, many labourers were laid off during heavy rain or snow. With little or no job security, often hired labourers in parishes along the coprolite belt who had been laid off after harvest would have been attracted by the higher wages offered by the coprolite contractors. Whilst some may have returned to farm work the stronger men would have been unwilling to return to lower paid farm work. In many cases farmers were compelled to raise the wages of the agricultural labourers to ensure their farm work was done which reduced their profits. This caused animosity and led to bad feeling between employers and labourers. Incendiarism was a common occurrence in this area with crops, barns and even farmhouses set alight. Although the local press reported such cases there was no evidence of any coprolite diggers being involved. In fact they had better job security as demand for coprolites was growing with the setting up of numerous manure manufactories around the country.

However, in nearby Exning, several years after wage improvements had been made in other parts of the country, there was discontent amongst agricultural labourers in early 1874 about low pay. This led them to consider combining into an Agricultural Union as had happened elsewhere. They went to the farmers demanding an extra shilling (£0.05) a week pay. The farmers refused. So, about 2,000 labourers went on strike. The farmers responded by locking out their labourers and refusing to employ any Union labourers at all. Those in tied cottages were threatened with eviction and many families' very existence was in jeopardy. The situation got so intense as to merit coverage in the national press. This may have been due to local farming and land-owning MPs, like Mr Ball of Burwell, being involved.

These were the days of "Captain Swing", the supposed leader of the agricultural labourers. Many attacks on farmers' property were attributed to him and his followers. The local MP, Mr. Ball, must have been involved, probably supporting the farming members of this agricultural constituency. Frederick Gifford, a reporter from "The Times" was sent to cover the incident and attended a public meeting held at Newmarket. An extract from one of his articles shed light on the conflicting views of farmers and labourers but also included details of what was going on in the area.

"I do not think that a majority of farmers in the district would long resist the advance for which the men at Exning struck, and I am still more clearly of opinion, upon the lines they are now fighting, victory for the farmers will be more disastrous than defeat. The effect of the lockout, I believe, has been greatly to increase the strength of the Labourers' Union in the outlying villages.. A mere attempt to gain a mere shilling a week on the one side and a refusal of it on the other, would have produced nothing like the sympathy and dogged feeling among the labouring class not hitherto connected with the Union by a refusal to employ all Unionists. Such a policy is bitterly resented as a denial of "the right of us poor men to stand shoulder to shoulder and pluck up a bit." This was one man's way of putting it to me. "Our masters," said another, "will let us spend our two pence in getting drunk or in any other mischief, but we mustn't put it in the Union." Of course there is another point of view from which the lockout may be regarded as legitimate defensive warfare by the farmers. The men, however, cannot be made, or perhaps expected, to look at it from any point of view but their own, and if the wholesale notices served on them to leave their cottages take effect, the exasperation and sense of wrong among them and their fellows for miles round will be such as one hardly likes to look forward to. Some hundreds of labourers are employed in the Fens of Cambridgeshire in Coprolite digging, and this comparatively new industry competes with husbandry for labour. In Burwell, a parish adjoining the Exning, I visited some of these diggings today on land belonging to Mr. Stephenson. The coprolites are a mass of petrified dung of extinct reptilia, found in the green sandstone formation, often mingled with bones and fossils. The surface soil where they are met with is black peat, which is about a foot deep. The coprolites lie here at a depth of six or eight feet, in layers about six inches thick, above the stiff blue clay, here called "gault." Fen land, the fee of which used to be

worth less than 10/- an acre, now lets at the mere privilege of winning the coprolite at from 70l. to 200l. an acre. When it is dug into the peat topping is put carefully aside, and after the coprolites are extracted the ground is levelled and the peat mixed with the new surface soil. This made land - the local name for which is "slurry land" - is then worth 10/- more an acre as arable land than it was before. The coprolites are carefully washed to free them from the clay, and come out then like bits of blackish stone, generally rounded, from the size of a cherry stone to a pigeon's egg, sometimes bigger. They are valuable as manure, and in a factory close by, belonging to Mr. Ball, the son of the late member for Cambridgeshire, I saw the process of conversion. They are ground in mills to a very fine powder; but this is valueless for manure until it has been mixed with sulphuric acid, when the product becomes a soluble superphosphate, and is worth about 55s a ton. The coprolite diggers earn 17s or 18s a week, and at harvest time desert the diggings for the farm. They are in fact agricultural labourers; but the work is much harder than that of the ordinary farm hand, though the hours are shorter and there is a Saturday half-holyday. The result, I am told, is that the number of recruits is small, and that the farm hands who have tried the work often go back to their old occupation at 13s a week. Another local industry is pursued by the Fen men, who dig peat for fuel or cut sedge for thatching, and are said to earn in this way an average of 20s. a week. The farmers say that the existence of these two industries in the district side by side with that of agriculture proves that the rate of wages paid to the farm hands must be a fair market rate, otherwise the farm hands would seek these two employments more readily than they do. The coprolite diggers are now turning Unionists. I may add that the Fen land in Burwell, where the coprolites are won, forms part of the Great Bedford Level. There is a navigable cut into *the Cam, and the land is kept drained by pumping engines, the cost of which is defrayed by a drainage rate."*

(The Times, April 16th 1874)

This was one of only two references to the Unionism of the diggers that has come to light. The local media, owned as it would have been at the time by the wealthier classes, would not have published stories encouraging strikes. A small independent newspaper in Bedfordshire reported a strike at coprolite works at Ashwell, Herts. (*Potton Journal*, June 17th, 1871). This resulted in the diggers being given increased wages but, interestingly, there was no mention of it in the *Cambridge Chronicle*, the *Cambridge Independent Press* or the *Royston Crow*.) Wages did increase during the early-1870s and with improved education and the availability of various publications there was an increased awareness amongst the working population about different wage levels in various parts of the country.

Gifford's article compared Burwell very favourably with the sheep farming area of Exning where labourers generally lived in little more than hovels. In Burwell two and three-bedroomed cottages with gardens were common. Demand for allotments was high with some farmers charging six pounds an acre for families to keep a pig and grow their own vegetables. This was 300% more than the highest agricultural rent!

There were some people in the area who argued that outside agents had been sent from the Midlands to encourage the labourers to strike. One farmer from Kirtling reported receiving the following letter.

"Mr turner, you think you are going to friten us, you will friten yorself if you don't mind, and so will all farmers. Fairst week all we men are out of work we shall com upon you we be gen as we mean to go on. Your head will be taken off firs. We will make a smash the first week we

are at ticket we cut off your head and set fire to your farms and we go rite thro the place, so you may look out for we mean to do it."

(The Times, April 16th 1874)

Others felt that the labourers were otherwise a happy and contented lot but one woman, Augusta Stradbroke, seemingly had not spoken to the same farm labourers as Gifford as she wrote,

"The men are offered 17s. and 18s. a week all the year round, and have declined making more than that at the present rate of weekly wages and the extra pay given for hay and harvest. You make no mention, and probably have never taken into account, the low rent of their cottages. For good houses with three bedrooms, kitchen and parlour, and a quarter of an acre garden, they pay only 1s.9d. a week; for two bedrooms, 1s.6d. a week. Also you say nothing of their many Benefit Clubs, clothing, coal and shoes &c., subscribed to unanimously and chiefly supported by their employers; their cottage garden shows and prizes; their dinners and treats at Christmas and harvest schools for their children, which until the passing of the late Act, were kept up entirely, and many are still, by their employers and landlords. All these are benefits and comforts which are not thought of, and would not be feasible in large manufacturing districts, but which add materially to the happiness and unity of the two classes, - labourers and employers." (Ibid.)

Harvest treats had generally declined in many villages in favour of cash payments and otherwise they were generally for the women and children. Benefit Clubs were clearly thought of as a boon to the labouring classes but one labourer called out of the field by the farmer to answer Gifford's questions felt otherwise.

"How old are you, John?" "Sixty-one next birthday, Master." "How many children have you had?" "Twelve - nine living." You have always kept them without help from the parish?" "Yes -Thank God; I never had a penny from the parish in my life." The man, as I afterwards found out, had received a small money prize from the village Agricultural Society for bringing up a family without parochial relief, and he was now earning the usual 13s. a week." How long did you subscribe to that benefit club of yours, John?" - "Nigh upon five-and-thirty years." "It's gone now has it not?" - "Ah, Yes! That was a bitter bad job surely!" This poor man-happily still hale and strong - had paid into the club 1s.6d. a month out of his hard earnings - by what extraordinary thrift and self-denial one may easily imagine with his large family - and now all was lost. But for the sentiment of the thing he might as well have been idle and improvident; and if the children for whom he had worked so hard could not support him his only prospect in old age was the workhouse. The club had "broke-up," and he tried to tell us how and why. The story need not be repeated; but that, said my companion, "is the history of three-fourths of the benefit clubs about here." (Ibid.)

With *The Times* reporting on it the circumstances must have been discussed by many across the country. The National Agricultural Labourers' Union held a meeting in Birmingham to discuss the event and its president, Joseph Arch, pointed out the justice of the labourers case. A cheque for £100 to help the men and their families was donated by Birmingham Trade Council and Arch, *"prophesied that unless the farmers soon recognised the rights of the labourer and conceded him justice the land would soon be left with none to till it."* The Union gave all the men 9s. a week from the subscriptions and actually encouraged those who wanted to emigrate, offering them free passage to Canada. (Ibid.)

Whether the farmers did succeed in evicting the families and ban Union labour or whether the men succeeded in getting their increase was not revealed. As there was no compensation for loss of work or accidents whilst working the men had to resort to helping each other.

The labourers had gained in confidence over the years and in May 1877 there was a meeting over in Waterbeach where Mr Arch, one of the leaders of the agricultural labourers, spoke. It attracted the attention of a reporter from the Cambridge Chronicle.

> "*WATERBEACH. LABOURERS MEETING addressed by Mr Arch who advocated the extension of the franchise to labourers and condemned the system by which the masters of workhouses were to get £5 for every one of their charges that were recruited into the army.*"

> (*Cambridge Chronicle*, 5th May 1877)

The manure manufacturers' demand for local phosphate accounted for the rapid exhaustion of this particular deposit by about 1875 as its shallow depth and proximity to the Cam, despite its low phosphate content, still made it worthwhile for farmers and contractors to extract. However, before the exhaustion of this particular deposit, a number of interested geologists paid visits to the many coprolite pits in the fens to acquire specimens and this led to further papers on the subject. Mr. T.G. Bonney was one such visitor. A professor at St. John's College, Cambridge, he reported that in this,

> "*...very profitable branch of industry... As much as £100 per acre has been paid for the privilidge* (sic) *of digging for them; formerly it used to be said that the work did not pay if the depth of the nodules exceeded 12 feet, but of late I have seen cuttings which went at least three yards deeper. The mode of*

proceeding is to dig a trench, with one face vertical, down to the nodule bed, to undermine this cliff, and then by driving wedges and crowbars along a line cut parallel to the edge of the cliff and some four feet from it, to split off a great slice of marl, and expose the stratum below. The marly seam, in which are embedded the glauconite grains and the phosphatic nodules, is then dug out and taken to a mill erected on the workings, where the mud is washed out, and the nodules are left behind, mixed perhaps with a little glauconite and a few larger stones. So free, however, is this bed from admixture with pebbles and other rock, that practically no hand picking is required.

(Bonney, T.G. (1875), *'Cambridgeshire Geology,'* pp.30-31)

By this time, any women and girls employed would have been a lot older as the 1870 Education Act in theory ensured younger children went to school. This loss of cheap labour would have increased costs. Farmers also suffered from this but, with practically no hand picking required, many women would have been laid off. By 1875, according to the geologist, Walter Keeping, *"the workings had been removed only 200-300 yards further off, where the bed rests on the Kimmeridge-clay."* (Keeping, W. (1875), 'On the Occurrence of Neocomian Sands with Phosphatic Nodules at Brickhill, Beds.' *Geol. Mag.* vol.11, p.374) In 1877 two further pits were referred to which could have been those referred to above.

"The road alongside its crest (if one may use the word), between the two pits, nowhere crosses the Neocomian beds. Two small shallow pits have indeed been opened adjoining the road on the west side, a little less than a quarter and half a mile respectively south of the northern pit."

(Bonney, T.G., (1877), 'The Coral Rag at Upware,' *Geol. Mag.* p.476)

The existence of the seam was used to increase the value of the 2,238-acre Soham Place Estate. There were extensive coprolite works in 1872 near Horsecrofts Farm and Longfields Farm where a one-inch bed was found 14 feet deep in 1872. Following the death of John Dobede on 1st December 1876 the estate was auctioned. The sale particulars mentioned that

> *"In the immediate vicinity coprolites are being obtained in large quantities, and they have been found upon portions of this property. It is confidently believed by experienced Coprolite workers that they may be a source of great profit to the owners of many of the lots included in these sale particulars."*
>
> (Cambridge Collection, CC.C06)

The "immediate vicinity" could refer to the two farms mentioned above. Unfortunately, there were the only references to diggings in Soham apart from in the 1891 census.

Some of the diggers on Fodder Fen must have realised that as the seam outcropped at the base of the ridge and dipped towards the river, it would similarly outcrop on the eastern side. In 1878 new workings were opened and, by 1879, plant and machinery had been set up in the fields about 500m. west of Spinney Abbey Farm, in the area of what is now Field Farm. (Keeping, H. (1883), 'Fossils of the Neocomian Deposits of Upware and Brickhill,' pp.1-2,72; Whitaker & Skertchley, (1891), 'On the Geology of Cambs. and Suffolk.' p.26; . O'Dell, I (1951), 'A Vanished Industry,' *Beds. Mag.* p.21.) Here, beneath 2m. of top and subsoil a similar high-yield seam 0.7m. thick was worked until about 1880. Another pit was worked in the 1880-81 period where, according to a visiting geologist, the coprolites were found between 1.7m. and 2.3m. deep in a gravelly sand of two and three feet in thickness which yielded 50% coprolite. Apparently, sixty barrow loads of sand yielded 3 cwt. of phosphatic nodules which were picked out after washing. Whilst it would have maintained employment for some, it would not have involved as many as a decade earlier. (Teall, (1875); Pennings and Jukes-Brown, (1881), 'Geology of Neighbourhood of Cambs.,' p.12; Woodward 1880??? or 1891 pp.28,102; Roberts, (1892), 'Jurassic Rocks of Cambs.,'; Reed, F.R.C. (1897), 'Handbook to Geology of Cambridge,' pp.30,62-71; Strahan, Flitt and Denham, (1919), 'Mineral Resources of Great Britain 1915-19', Mem. Geol. Surv. p.20)

This expansion was not mirrored elsewhere on the coprolite belt. The last four years of the 1870s were characterised by heavy rainfall and poor harvests. This had a serious effect on farming and also caused problems for the coprolite diggings. Higher water tables led to increased pumping costs. There were other problems though. The then Tory government had introduced Free Trade. This allowed the import of cheap meat and grain from the prairies of North America and the Pampas of South America which flooded the European markets. Prices fell and what has been called the "Agricultural Depression" set in.

This reduced farmers' demand for fertilisers when they couldn't sell their own poor harvests. Their reduced demand had an effect of the manure manufacturers. This occurred at the same time as some of the bigger concerns were beginning to benefit from their investments overseas. They were importing increasing quantities of cheaper and better quality phosphates from their mines in Spain, Norway, Canada and the United States. Prices for coprolite dropped from £2.95 a ton in 1876 to as low as £1.45 a ton in 1879.

This dramatic fall left many farmers and contractors in great financial difficulties. They reacted by curtailing operations and laying off labour. How many workings in this area ceased is unknown but evidence from the census confirms that they declined dramatically. Whilst some labourers would have found work locally, either returning to agricultural work or using their newly acquired technological skills to find alternative employment, others must have been forced to migrate.

According to the local historian, Richard Grove, there was some employment offered in the form of cement works that replaced coprolite works. (Grove, R. (1976), 'The Cambridgeshire Coprolite Mining Rush', p.47) However, many pits were left unfilled. Farmers or contractors would have been unable to afford the labour to fill them.

There were reports, however, of some workings continuing in the area. An extensive deposit was found which was worth extracting - even at these lower prices. The seam was 0.61m. - 0.92m. thick and less than 2.76m. below the surface. In 1880 it was being worked in pits east of Wicken church and south east of Bracks Farm (589712). (Worsam and Taylor, (1969), p.55; Whitaker, (1891), p.36) Whether they were still in operation the following year is not known.

The 1881 census reflected this Agricultural Depression. Wicken experienced a 25% drop in population, 289 people, since 1871. Amongst the 894 residents 36-year old Alfred Porter described himself as a "Coprolite raiser from 5a." He didn't say how many labourers he employed. Neither did 24-year old Genjar Nixon who was also termed a "Coprolite Raiser." There were only four coprolite labourers in the parish. They lived on Chapel Road, Drury Lane, Lower Drove and in Lode Cottage.

This decline was also noticeable in neighbouring parishes. Only one was recorded in Soham, Charles Hook, 26, of Pratt Street. He described himself as "Foreman of Works on Tramway." There were none in Stretham but, in Burwell, where Colchester and Ball had their manure works, there were thirty. The eldest was 36 and the youngest, 17. The average age was 27.5, considerably older than in 1871, which suggests the younger men had found alternative employment. There were no women or girls employed. The only one indirectly related was

Sarah Canham, 18, who described herself, as an "Ironstone labourer's wife."

The census provided the last evidence of the workings in Wicken. Whilst Porter and Nixon may well have continued their operations through the 1880s documentary evidence has not emerged. However, the closure of many diggings in the 1880s when American imports of phosphates restarted, the agricultural depression and resulting unemployment caused significant distress in many fenland parishes. The pressures on the parishes Poor Relief having to look after many destitute families and the accompanying out-migration of some families led some people to adopt philanthropic responses. For example, some landowners allowed their fields to be used as allotments and in Quy, Sarah Francis allowed a coprolite committee made up of unemployed men from Horningsea, Fen Ditton and Stow-cum-Quy to work the deposit under Quy Fen for nothing. There were workings in the Stretham area in 1891 but whether they had been continuous throughout the 1880s or restarted in the late-1880s is uncertain. In February 1891, hoping to capitalise on the revived interest there was the following auction of land in Soham.

> "SOHAM. Coprolites. -To be sold by private treaty, the coprolites contained in about 15 acres of land, within easy distance of two railway stations. Good vein. Cambridge Coprolites. Enquire of Mr. F.A. Johnson, Hall, Soham."

(*Cambridge Chronicle*,21st Feb.1891, p.1)

It is unknown whether the plot was worked but, although the diggings were only a short-lived occupation they must have provided a tremendous economic boost to the village and temporarily reduced the drift to the towns that became more noticeable towards the end of the century.

> "STRETHAM. Work stopped because of rain. -Farmers and their prospects. At last we have had a few fine days

which has enabled the farmers to get on the land once more, but, considering the state of the heavy lands, work is very much behind, and wheat sowing must be late. Although we have had a great deal of rain we have not suffered from floods as some parts have done. The coprolite pits were stopped for a few days but the men are working again, and have been all week. These small works are a great boon to the village, as they just employ all the surplus labour, which otherwise would be out of work during the winter."

(*Cambridge Independent Press*,7th November 1891
p7.)

The bed was also worked on a small scale in Stuntney sometime before 1892. Geological reports suggest that they were extracted from the sands which cap the hill on which the village stands. They were also reported as scattered in the fields on either side of the road, a mile southeast of the village, and by Ley Clerks Farm, east southeast of the village near Nornea. Whether they were worked here is uncertain. (Whitaker 1891,p.28; Roberts 1892 p.65. K. Oakley, British Phosphates, Wartime Pamphlets,Vol.8 no.3.)

When the diggings finally ceased is unknown. In 1894 the Quarry Act stipulated that any pit deeper than 25 feet had to incorporate strict health and safety regulations. These would have increased costs considerably. At the turn of the century Marr and Shipley, in their account of the natural history of the Cambridgeshire area, pointed out that,

"Around the Upware "island" a thin representative of the Lower Greensand occurs. Its greatest thickness is not much more than 10ft., but the locality was unsurpassed for fossils and phosphates. Unfortunately, phosphate working has

come to an end at Upware and Wicken and the only available exposure of these interesting beds is that furnished by a shallow ditch of the east side of the green road that runs from the south to the north pit at Upware. The best exposure is about 300 yds. north of the south pit, where occasional oysters can be collected. The section at the river entrance to the south main pit when dry shows the relations of the beds rather well."

(Marr, J.E.& Shipley, A.E. (1904), *'Handbook to the Natural History of Cambs.'*, p.23)

This latter pit is quite likely the Commissioner's Pit (GR.539708), which can still be seen today overgrown by trees just to the north of the village. Maybe this is the only evidence of an industry that must have provided many local families with a significant boost to their income and an escape from the traditional farm labour which had dominated the area for centuries.

During the Second World War, a study was made of potential sources of British phosphates and a detailed examination of the workings around Stretham and Little Thetford was made. Using books and papers on the area's geology the location of many of the diggings was described. (1inch O.S. 51N.W.; N.S.188; K. Oakley, British Phosphates, Wartime Pamphlets, Vol.8 no.3.(see fig.5) Prior to 1874 the deposit was found west of Manor Farm (Plantation House). The coprolites were found scattered through the sand with black Lydite pebbles and fragments of ironstone. Another pit at the south end of the spur, a quarter of a mile to the south-west was worked before 1875. Nine feet of sands and sandstone were completely removed to obtain the bed. This working is the site of the present sewage works. Further east there were pits in what was called Hundred Acres field. (Teall (1875),p.24; Whitaker and Skertchley, (1891), 'On the Geology of Cambs. and Suffolk,' p.21; 6 inch.Cambs.30SW.)

Other workings were noted under Middle Common, northeast of Stretham Ferry Bridge and a mile south of the church. These were worked between 1875 and 1883. Further east, on the other side of Green End Road, the largest operation took place but the geologists' reports gave no indication as to who was operating them, on whose land or who was purchasing them. (Whitaker 1891 p20.) Over seven acres were mentioned as being worked in the fen opposite Stretham Old Engine These were dug before 1891 and must have been a particularly profitable operation as the seam was found only two feet down. This would have entailed much lower labour costs. In some places pockets of coprolite were found lying on surface of the Kimmeridge clay. Just south of Little Thetford, on the left bank of Ouse, near the confluence of the Cam and Ouse, there were other workings in 1873. (6 inch Cambs.30S.W.) Here, beneath five feet of alluvium, sandy gravel was found with the coprolites in a seam 1ft.6ins. thick, resting on Kimmeridge Clay. (Skertchley (1877), p.253; Whitaker (1891), p.21.)

They were also worked along the line of Thetford Catchwater drain, about a mile S.S.W. of Little Thetford, towards Manor Farm. Spoil heaps from these workings were still visible as late as 1939. This suggests that the contractor may well have been the farmer himself who, when prices dropped during the agricultural depression so as to make it uneconomic, he failed to restore the land. On the south bank of the Ouse there were other workings under the fen, 1/5th mile below Stretham Ferry Bridge and more pits a little to the southwest. All of these were worked before 1882. In some cases, the bed reached 9 inches thick but dipped down to over 20 feet which must have curtailed the operations with extra labour costs. (6 inch Cambs.30 S.W.; Roberts, T., 'Jurassic Rocks of Cambs.', p.23. Whitaker 1891 p20.)

Their notes suggest there was a revival of the work between 1879-82 after which it seemed the import of foreign phosphates had brought prices down and demand disappeared. Map evidence, dated 1887, showed two disused Fossil Mills just east of Elford Closes in the 23-Acre field and not far from the Royal Oak.

(Camb 25' XXIX.16) This pub would have been well frequented by the diggers when the workings were in operation.

Little evidence remains today of the workings except the remains of a bank left when the work was finished (50767344 - 50977418) and perhaps some uneven fields where the land was not restored correctly. Unfortunately, the diggers destroyed evidence of Roman settlement in the area as in one set of diggings to the west of the road down Middle Common Drove, (513732) some pottery from that period was unearthed. (Cambs. Arch. 06877, 06905, 06928)

Most people are unaware of this unusual activity in this area during the latter half of the last century but the fossils can still be found on the fields and there was a report of a farmer raking them up, piling straw over them and igniting the heap, using the resulting white powder as additional fertilizer on the fields. The diggings brought this area of the fens a level of prosperity never experienced before or since. A number of manufacturing businesses profited from the demand for plant and machinery in the coprolite diggings. Much of the larger plant, pumps and steam engines etc. was either hired or purchased from large plant hire companies. One of Cambridge's iron founders, James Ind Headley, who built the famous Eagle steam engine, was very much involved in the coprolite business. He had his own coprolite works erected behind his Eagle Foundry on Mill Road in Cambridge and had his works, "*well fitted up to make the pumps, washmills, cast iron screens and steam engines to provide power.*" (Enid Porter's notebooks Cambridge Folk Museum 15/64-65) William Colchester established a chemical manure works, a brick works and a barge building works on Burwell lode. He also established an iron works in Bassingbourn where much of the coprolite plant and machinery was made. Small businesses like Kitchener's Iron Foundry in Potton supplied equipment to the coprolite contractors.

A lot of the equipment was steam-powered so coal merchants would have had good trade. The blacksmith would have had regular business from the coprolite works. Horses' shoes needed making and repairing. Whilst there would have been demand for crowbars, picks, shovels, spades and dog irons for supporting the planks, the major need was in repairs and sharpening. Picks used to wear out with all the picking out of the seam. Iron shovels, it was reported, used to wear out every fortnight! Maybe they lost their cutting edge. Cyril Croot, market gardener of Potton, claimed that they used to wear out after about three years. It probably depended upon what material was shovelled through. (O'Dell, I. notes on coprolite industry in Luton Museum)

Their business stimulated other trades. Local timber merchants and carpenters gained useful work in the erection and repair of coprolite sheds, making coprolite trucks and cutting timber for planks and supports. Carriers and carters would have made a good trade taking coprolites to the mills, wharves and railway stations. Barge owners similarly would have profited from the increased traffic. Surveyors, solicitors and auctioneers made good business out of the arrangements between landowners and contractors. Bankers would have profited from the loans made to speculators in the industry. The higher wages of the diggers would have provided a stimulus to the local economy. Local businesses would have profited and the public houses undoubtedly got good trade. Brewers saw increased consumption. Shopkeepers and other traders would have benefited from the increased spending power generated by the diggers, farmers and landowners.

There was increased demand for labour in the construction industry. Houses, cottages, farms and farm buildings were constructed, churches and chapels were built or renovated and much improvement was done during the coprolite years. The decline of the industry helps explain the out-migration in many parishes at the end of the century. What is surprising is the lack of photographic evidence. Perhaps other leases, correspondence and maps are still in a box in someone's attic. This story was entirely due to documents like these being stored and kept safe.

Researchers like myself have been able to piece together the varied pieces of the jigsaw to create an impression of an industry's growth, development and decline as well as the social and economic impact that it had on small agricultural communities. What was an unusual but small scale, labour intensive industry has been given little coverage in the local history books and this work has helped keep alive the memory of those local men, women, girls and boys who worked the pits. This book has helped put on record the lives of many people who lived, worked, played and prayed in the fens during the second half of the 19th century.

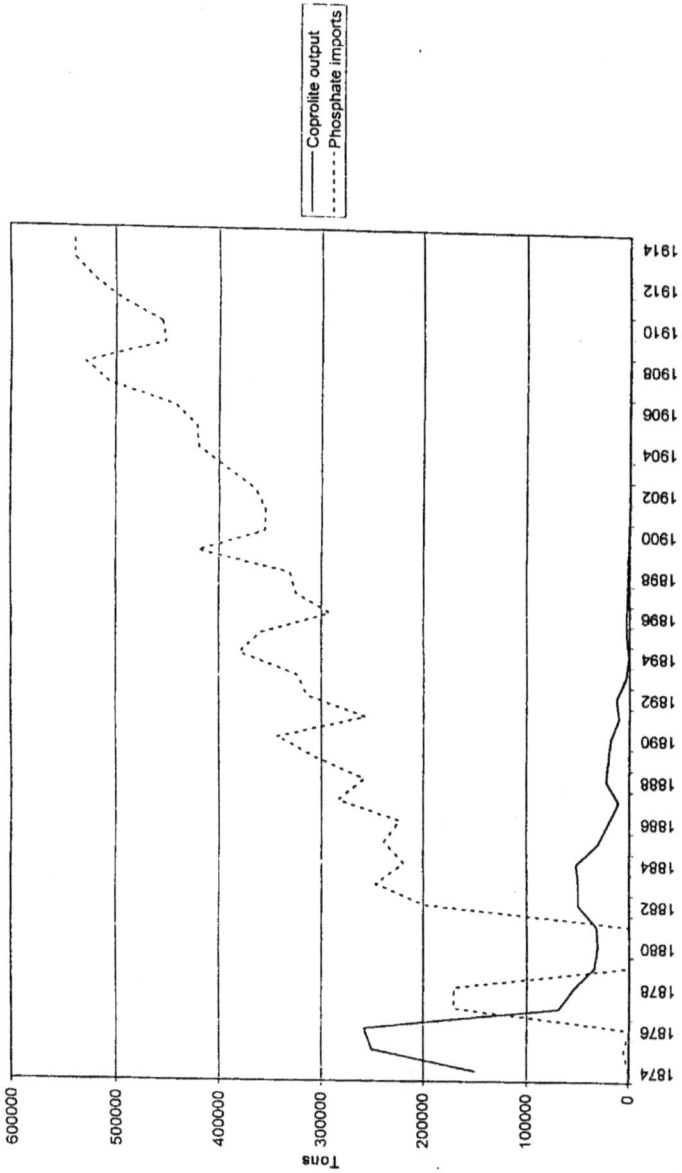

Coprolite Production and Phosphate Imports 1874-1914

www.ingramcontent.com/pod-product-compliance
Lightning Source LLC
Chambersburg PA
CBHW070108070426
42448CB00038B/2144